FINGERPRINT

SERIES

CHERIE SHIELDS

Copyright © 2017 by Cherie Shields

Fingerprint Series

All rights reserved. No part of this publication may be reproduced, distributed, or transmitted in any form or by any means, including photocopying, recording, or other electronic or mechanical methods, without the prior written permission of the publisher, except in the case of brief quotations embodied in critical reviews and certain other noncommercial uses permitted by copyright law. For permission requests, write to the publisher, addressed "Attention: Permissions Coordinator," at info@beyondpublishing.net

Quantity sales special discounts are available on quantity purchases by corporations, associations, and others. For details, contact the publisher at the address above.

Orders by U.S. trade bookstores and wholesalers. Email info@ BeyondPublishing.net

The Beyond Publishing Speakers Bureau can bring authors to your live event. For more information or to book an event contact the Beyond Publishing Speakers Bureau speak@BeyondPublishing.net

The Author can be reached directly BeyondPublishing.net/AuthorCherieShields

Manufactured and printed in the United States of America distributed globally by BeyondPublishing.net

BEYOND
PUBLISHING

New York | Los Angeles | London | Sydney
Library of Congress Control Number: 2017958056

10 9 8 7 6 5 4 3 2 1   9781-947-256-23-1

DEDICATION

I would like to dedicate this book not only to my husband, without whom I would not have accomplished this dream but also to my family. They taught me what it looks like to have a rooted faith with a life full of blessing and trials.

TABLE OF CONTENTS

1	Defining God	07
2	God, the Father	13
3	Our Relationship with God	19
4	Trusting God	24
5	Fruits of the Spirit	32
6	Prayer	43
7	How to Control Our Demons	48
8	How to Prepare for the Trials	58
9	Ways to Witness for Christ	63
10	Building a Relationship in God with Another	69

Fingerprint Series

CHAPTER ONE

Defining God

In the beginning, God created man and woman. In creating them, he designed us in his image, and, with that, came free will and a mind that exceeds that of any other creature. The way we are designed leads to two main points.

If you have ever walked into a room and instantly disliked someone, you'll know what I'm talking about. Whether it was tattoos, piercings, their style, the way they stood, or the way they laughed, we have all had that person who just rubbed us the wrong way.

The problem with that is…perception defines our mannerism. If we view someone as trouble, we treat them with caution. If we view them as arrogant, we steer clear or ignore their comments. Perception is so powerful that, when we predefine someone before knowing all the facts, we can ruin a great relationship, or force ourselves into a bad one. This is why what we think about God is so crucial in creating a relationship with Him.

How can you desire, seek, or serve someone you may perceive as "just there" or limited? It is human nature to want to define God, so we can understand Him. But, to understand Him, we must be with Him, and that will occur when we die. It is stated, "No eye has seen, no ear has heard, no heart has known all that I have in store."

To try would be to spend a lifetime in prayer with Him, because to know Him, you must spend time with Him. The one thing that makes followers of God different than any other religion is that we do not have rituals on how to get to heaven. We are simply taught to seek him.

Rituals—which I refer to as "formulas"—feed into the second largest portion of our human nature, which is routine. We like to know what comes next, list what needs to be done, and know the expectations before we start a task; but, with God, all limits are off, and His expectations are so high that we should never stop striving, which, at times, can be confusing and discouraging. While many religions strive to achieve favor in their god's eyes through rituals, God stresses church, prayer, and baptism but He never mentions what is to be done to achieve ultimate favor. To ease our own minds, we have created formulas to wrap our mind around what is needed. Formulas such as:

Church+ Prayer+ Baptism= Heaven

Reading Bible+ Prayer= Heaven

Prayer+ Serving= Heaven

I could go on, but you get the point. We have lost focus or never quite figured out the right perception of God. We placed God in a box that He never belonged in and created a perception with a ritual of how our faith should look, never thinking that our perception has limited our relationship and ability to know Him. To change our perception, we must redefine God. To do that is to redefine how we think. There are some common "types" of God that Louie Giglio did a sermon about:

- This is the invisible God. This God never shows himself; he is there as a reassurance and sense of distance peace. He does nothing but watch, and is simply a nameless, distant force.

- This is an Onstar God. This God who only assists in moments of need. He is a get-out-of-jail free card, and you tap into him only in particular moments. He can give directions and dispatch help.

- This is the Grandfather God. This God is there to spoil you. When he sees you, he gives you a dollar and takes you out for ice cream. He gives you everything you need to ensure you're happy.

- This is the Score-keeper God. This God acts as the coach of your life. He's always watching, critiquing, and seeing how you could do better. He has set the bar at varsity, but maks you feel like junior varsity level.

- This is the Doomsday God. This God is fire and brimstone. He's always out to get you. He feels we've all failed and has no tolerance.

- This is the Stained Glass God. This God exist only in Church, because it's the only time you think about him. He's in the back halls and only requires one day a week.

- This is the Me God. This God only wants happiness. His sole purpose is to make sure that you get whatever you desire. You just request it, and he provides, no matter what the consequence. It's all about you, and what you "want" and "need" are the same thing.

- This is the eBay God. This God is a genie in a bottle, and you only talk to him when you need something that is hard to get.

- This is the No God God. This is the God who doesn't exist. Even to deny him, you must say you don't believe in his name.

- This is the politically correct God. This is the God who loves everyone and doesn't judge. As long as you're a good person and are happy, He's happy and there is no hell.

The issue with these "God views" is that none of them fit God. God is all-knowing and omnipresent. He is loving and slow to anger, but the key is to see both sides of Him. He is always trying to reveal Himself to you. From before you were born, He had already formed you in the womb and started to show Himself to you, and continues to, through opportunities and trials He provides.

To help us better relate to Him, God took on the form of man in Jesus Christ. Through Jesus He modeled how to live and how to view God every day He was here. To understand Jesus, we must look at Romans 1: 4-5 which says "and who through the spirit of holiness was declared the power to be the Son of God by his resurrection from the dead: Jesus Christ our Lord. Through him and for his name's sake, we received grace and apostleship to call people from among all the Gentiles to obedience that comes from faith."

Jesus gave up Heaven to come to Earth as man, and the Bible regards Him in this way: Hebrew 1:1-4 "In the past God spoke to our ancestors through the prophets at many times and in various ways, but in these last days He has spoken to us by his Son, whom He appointed heir of all things, and through whom also He made the universe. The Son is the radiance of God's glory and the exact representation of his being, sustaining all things by his powerful word. After He had provided purification for sins, He sat down at the right hand of the Majesty in heaven. So He became as much superior to the angels as the name He has inherited is superior to theirs."

Jesus was God in human form. God could have chosen any way to come to Earth and reveal himself, but He came as a humble man. Jesus wanted to show us how to perceive God, and, out of all examples, He calls Him "Father." Jesus showed us how to have a relationship with God. One of the ways is baptism. In Mathew 3:17, after John baptizes Jesus, the heavens open up, and God says, "This is my beloved Son, and I am fully pleased with him." God knows the desires of our heart, and he knows we need to hear when we are loved. He calls Jesus his Beloved son. Not Son, not good son, not prodigal son…beloved. To be whole and unconditionally loved by a father is something every child longs for.

Jesus models a relationship again when He teaches us to pray. We have all heard the Lord's Prayer and even memorized it, but, when you take yourself out of the autopilot repeat, the will behind the prayer is humbling and challenging. It opens with "Our father, who art in heaven." A perfect picture is set for us. Not a king, not holy one, not almighty…simply father. This father is divine, and perfect. He is in heaven, the highest place distant for imperfection and pain.

Galatians 4:4-7 says,"But when the set time had fully come, God sent his Son, born of a woman, born under the law, to redeem those under the law, that we might receive adoption to sonship. Because you are his sons, God sent the Spirit of his Son into our hearts, the Spirit who calls out, "Abba, Father." So you are no longer a slave, but God's child; and since you are his child, God has made you also an heir."

Our first step in changing our perception is to understand that sin no longer holds us back. God sent Jesus to encounter every possible temptation, to display how we should act. In doing so, He showed us how we have a loving father, who no longer views us as sinners, but His children. We are a child of God bought with His blood. Once we surrender to God, He is no longer a distance figure but Abba, which is an Aramaic word meaning "dear father."

It's hard to connect with a faceless, voiceless thing, but we look at it all wrong. Louie Giglio does two amazing videos on God called "Indescribable" and "How Great is Our God." If you have the chance, take the forty-five minutes to watch them on YouTube, and see how much it resizes who God is. We're not talking about a shy, timid man. We are talking about a God who breaths stars. Stars that our sun could not compare to. This is the God who laid the foundation of the earth by speaking and holds the constellations in his hand. How easily we forget this! We think "God, if you could do this…" When you catch yourself saying if, you've lost sight of Him. It's not a matter of if, but of His will. God, if it is your will.

James 4:14-15 says, "Yet you do not know what your life will be like tomorrow. You are just a vapor that appears for a little while and then vanishes away. Instead, you ought to say, "If the Lord wills, we will live and also do this or that." We desperately need to recognize God's capability. Not that we can understand him, but grasp that he can achieve anything according to His will.

DAILY INSPIRATIONS

- *Our perception determines our actions*
- *we cannot formulate God*
- *God is capable of all, but is it His will*

REFLECTIONS

Do you have a formula that makes you comfortable?

How big is God to you?

Fingerprint Series

CHAPTER TWO

God, the Father

It is human nature to respond to everything we experience, but how we respond is based on our perception. God made himself a figure that we are all so familiar with; however, not all of us have the greatest views of fathers. Satan has worked hard to destroy families. America, in particular, is flooded with technology to tempt us, freedom that gives us comfort to divorce, and the comfort to forget how to practice faith because there doesn't seem to be a need.

Biblically speaking, a father is to be the head of a household, a spiritual leader, and a Jesus figure. He is to love his wife as Christ loved the church so how do you make God appear unobtainable? Simply remove the spiritual leader and make him appear broken in society. Then the preconceived of our earthly father will spill into our spiritual view thus disabling us and causing premeditated doubt and subconscious lack of faith as we come into God's presence. This view can be uncomfortable and frustrating, but God's only desire was to appear as a spiritual leader, advice-giver, provider in all aspects, and the one earthly figure that does all this is a father.

In the Old Testament, because we were separated from God by sin, you see how coming into the presence of God was an ordeal of sacrifice and special areas. To break these rituals which made Him appear unobtainable, God sent His Son to show us how to view Him and talk to Him. Jesus did this to help show us how to quench our thirst for acceptance and approval. This need for approval will not be satisfied by earthly things, but achieved through spiritual growth of accepting God as our heavenly father. All the parties, alcohol, drugs, and partners in the world cannot fulfill what God has designed.

There are four things we need to fulfill our desire of a father's blessing:

1. Love. We are designed to be loved. We thirst for it. We want to know, hear, and have it proven to us time and time again. A constant reassurance that were known and accepted.

2. Acceptance and approval. We each long for an unwavering support that he will accept us through each decision we make, whether good or bad. We want a father that we don't always have to ask permission to do everything, but rather our decisions make us unique. We want to be loved for our unique individual personality. There will always be a longing to be loved because you are different, and we want to hear that our differences is what he loves about us.

3. Participation. It doesn't stop at him just loving our uniqueness, he needs to participate. There's nothing worse than being in a big race and not having your dad show up to cheer you on. In this race of life, our heavenly Father seeks active participation. He longs to guide and direct you while giving you peace and joy. But to achieve that you must spend time with Him. I know I sound like a broken record, but one hour a week is not enough. If you only talked to your best friend one hour a week how close can you be? How much do you value their opinion? He desires to be there, but you must allow Him.

4. Peace. When you allow him to participate, he will breathe peace into you. He will let you know how much he believes in you. He will open doors of opportunity and show you that you WILL succeed. That you can accomplish bigger dreams than you have now.

Maybe you think these four things sound crazy. That love, acceptance, participation, and peace can be found here on Earth. I would dare you to try. The love of a spouse is amazing, but I don't want you to waste another minute. I dare you to give God a chance. We demand these four things from the people on Earth; why not try a heavenly Father? He only asks the same thing in return.

Some people think they don't need it. You may come from a broken or dysfunctional and maybe convinced yourself that you don't need it. You try to protect yourself from feeling vulnerable or feeling pain. Maybe you don't want to grasp Him as Father. Flesh will always disappoint you, but you don't have only one father who can fulfill your needs. We live in a broken world. Satan lives among us and wants nothing more than to destroy our destiny by destroying our image of God. So, what better way than to destroy our image? If you want to break a child's ability to communicate and respond well with God, then, destroy the image of a father. Even if it is broken, God can repair it. The Word of God gives life and restores trust that has been broken. 1 John 3:1 says, "How great is the love the father has lavished on us, that we should be called children of God! And that is what youi are!"

We are children of God. We are not given conditions or stipulations. We are not forgotten, abandoned, nor alone. We were bought with His son's blood, so that we could be called His Children. Nothing can separate us from that. 1 John 3:1 says, "The reason the world does not know us is that it did not know him. 2 Dear friends, we are children of God, and what we will be has not yet been made known." I love that! We are children on earth and when our spirit leaves our flesh what we will be is not even imaginable!

If you read Malachi 4: 5-6, his last words before there was 400 years of silence and Christ came were, "See, I will send you the prophet Elijah before that great and dreadful day of the Lord comes. He will turn the hearts of the fathers to their children, and the hearts of the children to their fathers; or else I will come and strike the land with a curse." God has always stressed the emphasis of a strong father

Fingerprint Series

figure. However, even in biblical times, they lost this. In Luke 1:17, it says, "And he (speaking of John the Baptist) will go on before the Lord, in the spirit and power of Elijah, to turn the hearts of the fathers to their children and the disobedient to the wisdom of the righteous-to make ready a people prepared for the Lord."

We all have a dad; the question is which one is yours. The empowering father? The type of dad who loves you unconditionally, but is not afraid to let you know when you've crossed a line. Is your father abusive? He tears you down, whether he does so physically, emotionally, or verbally. He always ready to take that cheap shot, and, in doing so, makes you always think you are wrong, creating a lack of trust in yourself or a father figure. Maybe you have the absent father. He left, or passed, or you did not see him after the divorce. Maybe he appears uneasy to talk to, or you sense an insecurity in him. Then, there's the passive father. He tries really hard, but he can never seem to quite pull it together. He doesn't wear the pants in the relationship, and anger is often a result. Often, it leaves the son feeling he will need to step up and be the man. Or is your dad performance-based? You get to hear the words "I love you" or "I'm proud of you" by earning them, through a series of tasks; grades, sports, or things around the home. This creates a child who is very competitive. They must win, because they are fighting for more than a trophy at a sports game. They fight for affection and acceptance. This is dangerous, though, because it creates a mentality that God helps those who help themselves. Rather than placing your trust in God and looking for his opportunities, you tend to go after what you want and think God will just open the door. What you "want" and what is "needed" are two very different things.

For those who have the all-star dad, trusting God comes easier. No matter how great your dad is, he is not God. Eventually, we all learn our father is not Superman, and that moment is devastating. Our earthly father is a reflection of God's design. However, God is the bigger and better version. He is not a reflection of your father; he is the perfection of your father. Mathew 7:7-10 "Ask, and it will be given to you; seek, and you will find; knock, and it will be opened to you. For everyone who asks receives, and the one who seeks finds, and to the one who knocks it will be opened. Or which one of you, if his son asks him for bread, will give him a stone? Or if he asks for a fish, will give him a serpent? If you then, who are evil, know how to give good gifts to your children, how much more will your Father who is in heaven give good things to those who ask him!"

If an Earthly father has the capability to love and care for you, how much more can your heavenly father offer? He is all-knowing and omnipresent, and He designed you. Each desire, weakness, and skill you have, He has placed in your heart with purpose. God has no issues, no ego, no insecurity, no anger, no fear. Everything you say is heard. Everything you go through, he understands. Only he can offer a peace that is indescribable.

Your family tree may be broken, you may not receive love from a father with anger issues, or you may receive love from an amazing father. Either way, you must see a new tree. A heavenly father may not be the head of your household, but He can be the leader of your heart. He waits to pour a love and a blessing over you. To show you the purpose of your life. If you come from a challenging household, you may ask how God can fix that tree. When I was at a Christmas tea, I heard Sheri Rose speak on how an invisible God becomes visible. The answer is this: when God restores you, and He always does, He fixes a broken family tree. When you show love to a father who is a drunk. When you pray over a father who struggles with anger. When you love your child with an unconditional support you never had.

I've seen God change the hearts of people around me, giving me the grace and compassion to love, even when it destroyed me. To forgive those who betrayed me and attempted to hold me down. This does not happen overnight, sometimes, I does not even happen over the course of weeks, but I urge you to never stop praying for them and for yourself. We will touch on this more in the prayer chapter.

Walk away tonight, and take time to process that you are a part of a new tree, and can start your own legacy. He waits to pour blessing upon you, His beloved son or daughter. He wants to help heal the wounds and strengthen the weak areas of your life. Most of all, He wants to bless you as your perfect heavenly Father.

DAILY INSPIRATIONS

- *Do you view God as a father?*
- *We all desire love, acceptance, participation, and faith*
- *You have a new legacy to find*

REFLECTIONS

What type of father do you have?

What good qualities are in your family tree?

What areas could you seek God in to show your family His love?

Fingerprint Series

CHAPTER THREE

Our Relationship with God

We have redefined God as all-knowing as well as all-powerful, and changed your lens to see him as a father. You have been adopted by the cross. Now, you must re-sculpt your relationship with Him. Ultimately, our relationship with God will affect how our relationships with others.

Take a moment, and think carefully about what I'm about to ask: What kind of relationship do you have with God? How often do you need to talk to Him? To spend time with Him?

Is He your best friend? Do you need to talk to Him every day? You need to spend time letting him know your accomplishments and struggles. Do you allow Him to know everything?

Or is He a good friend? Someone you talk to, but not that often. There is comfort in knowing they're there, and that you can call them randomly to say hi and hang out. You talk to them, but you don't let them all the way in. You don't need that kind of vulnerability.

Is He an acquaintance? Someone you only see on a rare occasion, such as Easter or Christmas. Other than that, though, you know each other's names, and that's enough. Someone you talk to only because you feel required. They are part of a routine, but they ultimately know little to nothing about you.

Is He a stranger? Is He the homeless guy by the freeway exit you see and give a dollar to out of kindness? You've seen Him around, but you have no desire to talk to Him or get to know Him.

Think long and hard, and be honest with yourself. You don't have to tell anyone which level of relationship you have with God. But our greatest weapon is knowledge. To know our weaknesses. I don't ask this to tear you down, but encourage you to fight the most common human instinct…comfortability.

The thing about God is: there is no structure on how to spend time with God, but you should feel a *need* to spend time with Him. Church, Bible, prayer, worship, silence…they all work. I can be just as guilty as anyone of neglecting my relationship with God. When I get home after a long day, and the DVR has my favorite shows, I often give in to the distractions. They provide temporary relief from the stress and worries of the day. But, when I pause to even spend just five minutes and put on a few worship songs as I cook, clean, or shower, I have peace restored, and am ready to get up and fight again.

I find when the Spirit moves in those quite moments, I realize how unworthy I am to talk to God, I am so humbled to find myself able to spend a moment with Him. Back when Moses was receiving the Ten Commandments, he had a special tent far outside of camp, where he could go meet God face-to-face. There would be sacrifices, and everyone would stop, in awe of the fact Moses was *speaking* to God, like a friend. Today, we are honored with the privilege of talking to Him, without all the ritual, and, rather than taking even five minutes a day, we say we can't make time. We have lost the Awe of God.

How can a father correct, teach, or be with his child if they are always too busy? He will create trials and challenges, until you take a moment to recognize who is really in control. It is not a punishment; it's tough love. I read a quote that said, "Sometimes, God takes us to rock bottom, so we can see that He is the rock at the bottom." We hear the word "God" so many times that we have dulled ourselves to the importance of who God is!

I had the opportunity to hear Francis Chan speak at a recent conference, and something he said absolutely paralyzed me. Today, we get so caught up with our speakers, our teachers, and disciples of the Bible, and we are so in awe that for some reason, we forget who put them there. The one who controls it all! Think about this: if you had a special tent that was designated by God, and the only time you could talk to Him was from that tent, and you put that tent in your family room or garage, how many times could you walk past it and say, "Nope. Not today. Sorry, I'm too busy." am willing to bet you wouldn't. Seeing that tent as a holy place housed for speaking to God…it paralyzed me. It shattered my view of prayer and helped me refocus on the greatness of my Father.

So why is it so hard to just "be" with God? One of the hardest things I still work on to this day is being with Him. Just being there ready to hear Him. I won't lie: this is the hardest thing! It cans seem almost impossible to sit in silence, when my thoughts are going over everything I need to do; the functions of the upcoming week, and the shows that beckon me to watch them. On top of all this, I have a dog (some may have children) that makes it impossible sit anywhere without being needed. Satan is wise, and all these are used to hinder your sensitivity to hear God.

1 Peter 1:13 advises, "So think clearly and exercise self-control. Look forward to the gracious salvation that will come to you when Jesus Christ is revealed to the world." In other versions, they say sober-minded. Meaning without distraction, nor under influence. The choice of self-control is distinctly chosen to show the issues with coming to God while falling asleep, or interrupting prayer with checklist.

God does not force you to hear him. He speaks softly, so only the hearts that seek him can hear. Even to His most loyal disciples, God chose to speak through softness. Just like in 1 Kings 19:11-12, "So He said, "Go forth and stand on the mountain before the LORD."

Fingerprint Series

And behold, the LORD was passing by! And a great and strong wind was rending the mountains and breaking in pieces the rocks before the LORD; but the LORD was not in the wind. And after the wind an earthquake, but the LORD was not in the earthquake. After the earthquake a fire, but the LORD was not in the fire; and after the fire a sound of a gentle whisper."

Why spend time with God? The answer is this: the more time you spend with HIM, the faster you allow Him to get rid of the wounds, stress, and insecurity you carry. When it comes to healing an emotional wound, you have three options:

1. You can put a Band-Aid on it, and cover it up-shame and regret commonly force us to do this.

2. You can deny it. A pride complex may lead you to believe you are too amazing to fail.

3. Or, you can stitch it. This is the most painful way to heal a wound. However, by doing so, you allow yourself the quickest path to healing, by acknowledging the pain and letting it go.

Like any relationship in your life, what you put into it, is what you will get out of it. Think back to the answer you gave earlier. If you do not spend time with God, you cannot expect to know Him or feel Him. Many people are under an illusion that Followers of God have a carefree, hippie attitude, and have no issues, and everything is great. It is actually quite the opposite.

One of my biggest pet peeves is when people make t seem to easy to "be" with God. It's not! I'm tired, distraced, and can become super frustrated. People would tell me what worked for them, but that does not mean it's a guaranteed fit. Some will say, "oh you need to get up in the morning and read the Bible before you start yoru day." Others say you need to sit on the floor, or pray in silence in a dark room. Those are all great, but there is no one way. I wake up at 4 a.m. everyday so no I'm not getting up any earlier. When I read The Bible I feel like I am reading some foreign language sometimes. I could read a whole chapter and think, "ok what was I supposed to get out of that?" Honestly, most people have a hard time reading the Bible. So how do you deal with that? Simple! With technology we have so many avenues to help us. Giving up is talking the easy way out. In the morning I listed to K-Wave, these brief twenty minute sermons every thirty minutes is perfect. Not too much, and can get me started for my day. If not sermons, then put on some worship songs as you drive to work. Still not working? You can pray on your way to work. Praying while driving is always convenient for me. Still not working? You can download one of the thousands of apps that will send you a daily devotional every morning. You can also buy a daily devotional book. If you are in a serious relationship I highly recommend the devotional by Dr. James and Shirley Dobson called "Night Light." It has his and her questions that help you put into perspective your role in your relationship. The whole point is that if you can give God fifteen minutes a day through reading the Bible, devotional, worship, prayer, or listening to a sermon you will see an increase in your peace and joy throughout your day-to-day life.

DAILY INSPIRATIONS

- *God needs time to speak with you*
- *He can provide peace and joy*
- *He does not specify how to spend time with Him- it's individual to you!*

REFLECTIONS

How much time do you spend with God?

Is being with God hard for you?

What methods could you try to help hear God?

Fingerprint Series

CHAPTER FOUR

Trusting God

Trust is a difficult concept. By definition, it is reliance on the integrity, strength, ability, and surety, of a person or thing. Just like love, you can't touch it, force it, or create it, but, when it's destroyed, you can feel it.

Trust starts out easy when we are kids, but, as we grow older and experience heartbreak or disappointment, it becomes a harder concept. Instead, you begin to give the illusion you trust by showing a shallow version of yourself, or by keeping people at arms-length. Trusting people is hard enough, but, to trust a God you cannot see or hear can seem impossible. It can be challenging as you pray and feel nothing, as you worship and feel distracted.

I have gone my whole life knowing God and thinking I was trusting Him, but it turns out I wasn't. It wasn't until I was twenty years old that I discovered what it means to trust God. The hardest part is that without trust, you cannot expect your relationship with God to grow or open doors, because, instead of being focused on your actual relationship with God, you are too focused on religious routines. When that happens, we end up going through motions that prove we believe in God, but that are still not trust. We will always have to challenge ourselves to step out in faith, because it is a concept that has been written about, but never mastered.

Just like the best things in life, things like trust, love, fulfillment, and God are not tangible. They leave impressions. For instance, think of a moment of pure thrill, nervousness, or overwhelming joy. Those moments remain so vivid that, even years down the road, you will hear a song or walk by a smell that will take you back to that place.

But, with everything that provides fulfillment comes risk. You have no way of knowing if the other person will love you back, or if your best friend will betray you, but, with God, you know He is always there. He is the same yesterday, today, and tomorrow.

How do you begin to trust God? It's not easy. It doesn't happen overnight, and, sometimes, it doesn't even happen for long periods of time. Here is the good news: the Lord is waiting on you, which means you control how quickly or slowly you learn to trust.

When I was twenty years old, I met Ben. We were on two different stages of life. I found him extremely attractive, but, other than that, he was the opposite of everything I was looking for. Somehow, I fell for him. I'll never forget the moment I was driving home from work and we had been dating for about a month and I was a mess. I pulled over on a side street, crying and angry with God, asking why I was falling for a man I could not be with! I told myself, *"I'm not going to get hurt again in another relationship that is a waste of time, and that was it!"* My mind told me I was done, but my heart was shattering and I didn't want to walk away. Which made me even madder! In a hurt anger, I challenged God. I told God that if He wants me with Ben, He needs to show me.

It started with going to church together every Sunday. When I asked Ben, he said okay, and had no problem with it. I was in shock. It was then that we began building our foundation as a couple in Christ. As time went on, I continued to challenge God in things I wanted to see in our relationship, and, sure enough, He always revealed it to me through things Ben would say or do.

Today, Ben and I have been married 5 years, and God still continues to grow us in ways I could not imagine. That is how I discovered

Fingerprint Series

my need to trust God. There is no easy guide, and it took months for me to overcome my doubts, but, every time I challenged God and watched, he delivered ten-fold. My life motto has become Proverbs 3:5-6, "Trust in the Lord with all thine heart; and lean not unto thine own understanding. In all thy ways acknowledge him, and he shall direct they path."

All this sounds good and enlightening, but there is a catch. Most of us are not going to like it. If you are going to trust God, you must be prepared to have the door open or shut. Just because I really wanted the relationship with Ben did not mean that God would build the foundation. I had to trust that God would either grow the relationship, or take it away, depending on *His* will. That was a killer.

This is why trust is so impossible at times: we convolute it with our will and expect God to conform. That is not the deal. God will meet you in your time of need and show you a path, but you must be prepared that it may not be one you want to take. The trust is knowing if you are praying over something you really want and you do not get it, God has a better opportunity where He wants you to be.

When you struggle with trusting God, remember He designed us with free will. Even better, He designed you, specifically. He made you unlike any other person. He knows your strengths and weaknesses, and, as long as you surrender them, He will use them for His glory in whatever position you find yourself, Proverbs 19:21, "Many are the plans in a man's heart, but it is the Lord's purpose that prevails."

My biggest personal fear is that my desires will block my ability to see the will of God and where He is calling me. The beauty of Proverbs is it tells us that no matter what you do, He has a plan that will work it all out. Sheri Rose, the author of *His Princess: Love Letters from Your King,* is as an amazing woman. When she won Miss America, she appeared to have the world by the tail but, one night feeling alone, she checked into a hotel room, prepared to kill herself. In that moment, she reached out to God and asked Him if He was real to meet her in that room. What happened next, she never could have guessed. God met her in that room, and, soon, He inspired her to write a book. She suffers from dyslexia and never had a dream to write. Now, she is a best-selling author, with over one million books sold. When you hear her speak, she often talks about how, because of her dyslexia, God has the ability to speak through her, because she doesn't get in the way. She had no idea what her life would hold stepping out in faith that day, but it led to touring with Extraordinary Women and being featured in a special by Billy Graham.

So often, we hear the stories of people who trust but only once they lost everything. Moses was in the desert, happily married with kids, when God came into his life and told him to go back to Egypt. What a lot of people don't know about Moses is he had a stutter. Moses did not view himself as strong or heroic. Yet, God choose him to go to Egypt and challenge Pharaoh. By the end of his argument with God, he had so much trust that he took his wife and son with him to Egypt!

As you step out with God, in trust for a job, health, or relationship, it will leave you vulnerable and feeling exposed. There are many emotions that will go with it, such as anger, frustration, confusion, and desperation, and those feelings are okay. Our human side will always come out when dealing with deep-seeded emotions. But, whatever you do…don't stop spending time with God. Spending time with God, wither a devotional, worship, or sermon, are the only way to strengthen your relationship and give you the trust necessary to step out into the unknown.

When I finally understood how to trust God, my life became incredibly clear and peaceful. I gained confidence in myself and began to pursue goals with a passion, because I understood my purpose. Until I learned trust, I had limited myself with what I call the "awe factor." I look at Christian authors, pastors, and the disciples with awe, thinking, *If only. If only I could hear God like they do. If only God met me in that quiet place. If only God would show me a miracle. Then, I could move mountains with only the faith of a mustard seed!*

That was the wrong focus. It is a great tactic used by Satan to convince us we are not faithful enough, trusted enough, or talented enough to be a part of God's plan. I struggled with this until I was changed by the story of Peter. We all know the disciple Peter, whose real name is Simon, to be a strong leader and great influencer. He helped found the Christian church, and converted thousands at a time by his teachings, but he was still human. There are two stories of his that completely changed my view and finally got me to break through the awe factor to see myself as a vessel for God.

The first was when Peter first saw Jesus walking on water, he decided to test Him and said, "If it is truly you, then, tell me to come." And Jesus called Peter out onto the water. Peter stepped outside of the boat and into the storm, his eyes fixed on Jesus. I couldn't imagine in that moment throwing my legs over the side of the boat in a huge storm and pushing off into the water. But, as he placed his feet on the water, he did not sink. He began to walk on the water toward Jesus! It wasn't until he began to focus on the storm and waves that he sank, and Jesus grabbed him.

Many criticize Peter for his lack of faith, but I am in awe of his faith. Peter is the only person, other than Jesus, to have walked on water. What I learned from Peter is that we can challenge God. It's okay to ask for a sign. It's okay to say, "God, open the door, if that's where you want me." Doubt is often part of the uneasiness of stepping out, but doubt is also a tool of Satan to paralyze us. Which is why we must stay focused, and push through the doubt and fear with prayer.

When my husband lost his job, he spent a few months looking for a new one. He'd had two previous jobs: one he ended up hating, but took for the pay. The other, he took thinking it was his dream job, but it was a worldly and unhealthy environment. When he got a call out of the blue for a job with a company he had never heard of in the technology world— which he wasn't really interested in— he hesitated. At the same time, he was also contacted by Mazda to work in their marketing department. My husband loves— no, is obsessed with— no, dreams about— cars!

He had the interview with the technology company set, and Mazda asked him for the same interview time. He prayed, asking God for a sign. My husband prayed that he would ask Mazda to change his appointment. If they said yes, we would see what happens. If they said no, he knew God was closing that door. Mazda ended up saying no, and my husband gave it up on the spot. The hiring manager was surprised and said he was the number one candidate, but God clearly answered and he had to accept it.

My husband took the job with the technology company unsure how he could do it, and is now thriving. He loves his job, and is so thankful to be in a company that is investing in him and allowing him to grow.

Satan will try and make you think you need to figure it out. He'll keep you up at night, running scenarios and contemplating pros and cons; don't get trapped. Doubt is human, but it can become sinking sand, paralyzing what God has in store. What many people do not understand is that Jesus was not disappointed that Peter fell. I believe God looks at us like a parent watching a child walk for the first time; you take a few steps and fall, but there is still the excitement and encouragement to try again. By taking those first few steps, you are starting toward freedom. For a child, it is the freedom to explore. For a believer, it is the freedom to find spiritual fulfillment, and a path that will leave you satisfied by walking with the Lord.

The second story was when Peter denied knowing Jesus three times the day Jesus was arrested and crucified. For those not familiar with Peter, he was so confident that he was convinced he would never do God wrong. He would never fail, nor deny God. He loved him too much! That quickly changes, and, when Peter denied Jesus, thus realizing his failure, he did what so many of us do when we fail. Peter returned to his old life of fishing, taking many of the followers of Jesus with him. He was so ashamed and disheartened that he retreated to punish himself. Thinking he could do and be nothing to Christ.

How often do we box ourselves in and allow shame, disappointment, or guilt keep us from getting up and trying again? It is another tactic of Satan to keep you from fulfilling your destiny. You retreat to the familiar. For some, that is an addiction. For others, it's a safe place of conformity.

Francis Chan has an amazing video on YouTube called "The Balance Beam." It sums up what so many followers of Christ do: live their life with a low level of risk in the safe place, until they can stand before God. What if you chose not to follow the norm? What if you chose to trust God just enough to walk on the balance beam?

Christine Caine was given up at birth, born in one of the poorest districts of Australia, and sexually abused for ten years. When she gave her life to Jesus, she started volunteering at the church, and was the only one to show up that day. After that, God opened the doors for her to be used. When she speaks, she will often say, "It's not about being qualified; it's just about showing up!" She is right.

In the case of Peter, Jesus showed up after a day of unsuccessful fishing. Jesus tells Peter and the other followers to cast their net on the other side of the boat. When they do, they are weighed down with the number of fish they catch. When Peter realizes who it is, he jumps off the ship and swims to Jesus. This moment was so pivotal for me, because it's exactly what so many do. We let God down, then, we retreat to safety to deal with our shame. When God shows up, we try to earn his forgiveness. We think if we can just prove ourselves, if we just volunteer extra at the church, it will get us back into the good graces of God. Yet we never left. Rather, we took ourselves out.

How many times have we done something similar, wherein we try to work away our guilt, shame, or disappointment? Thinking we can earn God's trust back. But what Jesus did next leaves me breathless. He asks Peter three times, "Do you love me?" Peter responds, "You know I do!" Then, Jesus says "…then, feed my sheep." At that moment, Jesus commissions Peter to become the head of the church. Jesus did not focus on his failures, He did not shame his lack of faith, rather, He embraced Peter with love and called him to a greater purpose. Because of that example, we now have so many stories of Peter that show us examples of what "Faith on Fire" looks like.

How do you become like Peter? Even if you don't preach to the masses, being there for one person can make a difference in their life. To achieve this kind of faith, you need to pray. Know the Word (even if it's just a quick devotional), and keep yourself in check. Remember that God is in control. Just keep reminding yourself He provides and will work all things— good or bad— for the good of His will. In the next few chapters, we will go over how to establish this trust through prayer, and how the enemy will work his hardest to destroy it.

Isaiah 45:3-4 says, "Listen to me, descendants of Jacob, all you who remain in Israel. I have cared for you since you were born. Yes, I carried you before you were born. I will be your God throughout your lifetime-until your hair is white with age. I made you, and I will care for you. I will carry you along and save you." We serve a God who knows us intimately and will place us in the perfect place, even if we haven't dreamed of it yet.

DAILY INSPIRATIONS

- *To have faith is to trust God*
- *Trust brings peace*
- *Doubt is normal, but can become sinking sand*
- *You can challenge God, but then you must accept His answer*

REFLECTIONS

Have you been in a situation where you had to trust God?

Do you often pray when you feel doubt?

Do you recognize when you retreat from your faith?

Fingerprint Series

CHAPTER FIVE

Fruits of the Spirit

This chapter brings up a topic that will make many uncomfortable. We have all heard of the fruits of the spirit, but do we see them in our lives? When you decide to give your life to God, something changes in you. Your actions, motivation, and purpose become different than those of the rest of the world. You do not focus on things like money and possessions to make you happy. Now, you focus on your relationship with Him.

If you've ever been around a new believer, it is the most exhilarating thing to witness. They become so on fire for God, they are addicted. Like a new relationship, they eat, sleep, and drink it. As they do, changes in their life become evident. If you truly believe in God and have asked Him to take your life, this chapter should come naturally. Being a follower of Christ isn't about just believing; it's about walking in Jesus' footsteps and living as an example for Him. When you do this, your life will naturally bear fruit.

This is where problems begin. It is a simple concept, but the enemy is good at twisting this to go to one extreme or another. On the one hand, as a believer, you become obsessed with this concept. You feel you need to have more fruit and begin to force it. On the other hand, you do not focus on your relationship and bear no fruit, because my relationship is "private" and doesn't need to be proven. Both sides will land you a slave to sin.

It sends a chill down my spine whenever I hear the quote, "If you were accused of being a (follower of Christ), would there be enough evidence to convict you?" I've been called many things for my faith. I have been criticized, cast out, and picked on, but the hardest moment in all these interactions came when I was in college.

I was assigned to a group project with a girl named Amber. We were waiting for the remainder of the group to show up, when someone wanted to spark a debate about God. I was talking to that person, when Amber stated how much she hated Christians. I asked her why, and she said, "You all are no better than me, and, yet, you judge me. You all smoke, do drugs, sleep around, and get drunk. Yet, because you ask for forgiveness, it makes it okay for you?" This is the age-old battle. The lukewarm believer that represents God, and, in their lack of testimony, does more damage than they could ever imagine.

I looked down and shook my head and said, "No. We are not better because we have God. Those people you speak of are not true believers. A study done in 2009 showed that seven out of ten people will call themselves a Christian because it was the faith associated with them growing up. Three out of those seven are truly practicing believers. It kills me to say this, but most 'believers' are not actually following Christ."

She proceeded to tell me a story of her best friend's dad, who cheated on her mom multiple times. When her friend and Amber asked him why he was doing that, he told them it was okay, because he confessed it to the priest and received forgiveness. Because of that man, Amber now resents all believers and God. I am very hard on myself for exactly this reason. So many people turn from God because of a bad experience in a church or with a "believer."

We are called and commissioned to preach God's word and live as an extension of Him. Many people will fight me on this and say, But *I'm a good person, and that's what is needed.* I challenge you to find in the Bible where it says if you are good you are saved. That is 100 percent a lie. Look at a fruit tree as an example. How can you tell what type of tree it is? You can tell by its fruit. When you look at an apple tree when it's in season, you don't think, *Oh, it grows lemons.* You also don't need to be an expert to tell. It is the same in our lives. When we follow Christ, we bear fruit, meaning: in trials, we have peace and patience; in hurt, we are able to forgive; in times of joy, we give glory to God and not ourselves.

John 15:1-2 says "I am the true vine, and my Father is the gardener. He cuts off every branch in me that bears no fruit, while every branch that does bear fruit he prunes so that it will be even more fruitful." This chapter is not one of my favorites. Jesus is explaining that if you are following Him, you bear fruit, and God will "prune" you to produce more. That means God is constantly at work in us, which is a trial. If you bear no fruit, God must let you go. He doesn't just cut you out of his life for fun, but the free will he gives us dictates if we will stay attached to Him or not. Many will take that verse and make God out to be heartless, but look at the parable in Luke 13:6-9 ," A man had a fig tree growing in his vineyard, and he went to look for fruit on it but did not find any. So he said to the man who took care of the vineyard, 'For three years now I've been coming to look for fruit on this fig tree and haven't found any. Cut it down! Why should it use up the soil?' 'Sir,' the man replied, 'leave it alone for one more year, and I'll dig around it and fertilize it. If it bears fruit next year, fine! If not, then cut it down.'"

Jesus does not tell us what happened. We do not know if the tree decided to bear fruit or was cut down. God is the man who owns the tree, but Jesus is the man pleading for another year. Ultimately, it our choice. I have always been different because of my faith. I don't believe in getting drunk, living together before marriage, nor sleeping together before marriage. Am I perfect? Absolutely not. I have failed more times than I can count, but I still strive to live a life that reflects the Son of God who walked this Earth to give me an example.

Why is bearing fruit so important? It shows that you are a believer. We need to recognize that we produce fruit, and that fruit can be inspected. In Matthew 7:16-20, it says, "By their fruit you will recognize them. Do people pick grapes from thornbushes, or figs from thistles? Likewise, every good tree bears good fruit, but a bad tree bears bad fruit. A good tree cannot bear bad fruit, and a bad tree cannot bear good fruit. Every tree that does not bear good fruit is cut down and thrown into the fire. Thus, by their fruit you will recognize them."

If you've been in a church, this is where it can start to go sideways. When you're around other believers, you feel pressure to perform and show your fruit. We start making "fake fruit" we can pull out when we need to display our "faith." This is so frustrating, because this is where so many people get a bad taste in their mouth for believers. We begin to compare ourselves to those around us and, even worse, judge others to make ourselves feel more accomplished.

We are all guilty of it to some degree. It's human nature to feel jealous. Jesus did not come and die to free us from sin for us to become slaves to doing good works. Good works should come naturally, and you should want to do them out of appreciation to God, but doing good works doesn't save you! In verses 22-23 of the same chapter, it says, "Not everyone who says to me, 'Lord, Lord,' will enter the kingdom of heaven, but only the one who does the will of my Father who is in heaven. Many will say to me on that day, 'Lord, Lord, did we not prophesy in your name and in your name drive out demons and in your name perform many miracles?' Then I will tell them plainly, 'I never knew you. Away from me, you evildoers!'"

These verses are directly talking about "religion." There are many false prophets who speak in the Lord's name, but do not have good intentions. How will you know if they can be trusted? By looking at their lives. Seeing if their life reflects Jesus' example.

If you listen to many of the more recognizable names today, such as Greg Laurie, they will openly state they hate religion. Religion is manmade, and is not perfect. God made following Him simple: repent, keep the commandments, and seek Him first. Is that easy?

Absolutely not. Volunteering so many times a week, reading the Bible every day, and feeling we must pray so many times each day weighs us down with "musts". We must do this; we must do that.

It all goes back to our human nature of following a formula to check the box and be saved. It doesn't exist! Seek God…the rest will happen. That's it! You want the truth? Here it is: The world has the right to look at the church and us and judge us. We are called to be the example, and, if we are not showing fruit, it shows we are not right with God.

Fruit can be inspected by God and others; however, it cannot be manufactured. In John 15:4-8, it says, " Remain in me, as I also remain in you. No branch can bear fruit by itself; it must remain in the vine. Neither can you bear fruit unless you remain in me. "I am the vine; you are the branches. If you remain in me and I in you, you will bear much fruit; apart from me you can do nothing. If you do not remain in me, you are like a branch that is thrown away and withers; such branches are picked up, thrown into the fire and burned. If you remain in me and my words remain in you, ask whatever you wish, and it will be done for you. This is to my Father's glory, that you bear much fruit, showing yourselves to be my disciples."

The relief in this is that we do not need to worry about bearing the fruit. God states he will produce it. All we need to do is fertilize our heart. How do we do that? Through prayer, reading the Bible, listening to sermons, daily devotionals, and worship. The list goes on. Many will try and tell you to do x, y, and z, but, just because it works for them, doesn't necessarily mean it will work for you. I've been a believer my whole life and still have a hard time reading the Bible, so I do devotionals. I still read the Bible, so I cannot be deceived by the enemy, but not every morning at 5 a.m. in a quiet space, as some Christians might make us feel we ought to do. How does your tree bear fruit? By flesh, by works (religion), or by the Spirit?

What are the Fruits of the Spirit? Galations 5:16-26 says, "But I say, walk by the Spirit, and you will not gratify the desires of the flesh.

For the desires of the flesh are against the Spirit, and the desires of the Spirit are against the flesh, for these are opposed to each other, to keep you from doing the things you want to do. But if you are led by the Spirit, you are not under the law. Now the works of the flesh are evident: sexual immorality, impurity, sensuality, idolatry, sorcery, enmity, strife, jealousy, fits of anger, rivalries, dissensions, divisions, envy, drunkenness, orgies, and things like these. I warn you, as I warned you before, that those who do such things will not inherit the kingdom of God. But the fruit of the Spirit is love, joy, peace, patience, kindness, goodness, faithfulness, gentleness, self-control; against such things there is no law. And those who belong to Christ Jesus have crucified the flesh with its passions and desires. If we live by the Spirit, let us also keep in step with the Spirit. Let us not become conceited, provoking one another, envying one another."

The biggest one is love. Love is everything in your Faith. Everything about following God is dependent upon, stands on, and comes from the Love of God. If you do not have love, you do not have joy, peace, or grace. Love is the foundation. That is why you will hear God is love, *not* God loves. According to Paul in the Book of Romans, that love is the most powerful force in the Universe. It is more powerful than any other power at work in the Universe that is affecting our lives. It's more powerful than the flesh, than angels, than demons, than the past, than the future, than everything that is in heaven or earth. Nothing can draw a line that keeps us from knowing the Love of God. Nothing can separate you from the Love of God, if you choose to walk in truth.

In John 13, Jesus gives a new commandment: to love one another as I have loved you. Why this commandment? Because the old commandments showed us what we cannot do. But this shows us the direction of the New Covenant. It is not about what we cannot do, but what we are called to do. In this New Covenant, we are simply to love God and love people. This concept is simple, and leads into a much bigger picture. If you love someone, you will not harm that person, rather, you will serve that person.

In John 3:16, God showed the greatest action of love when He sent His son to die for us. Jesus laid down his life. Love is costly. We begin to learn that from a young age, when we lose a pet, start to have a crush, or even when a friend hurts us. Love comes naturally, but becomes hard when it's tested. When we need to do something we don't want to do. Anyone can love— that is easy— but that is why we are called to love our enemies. To live selflessly. It's easy to display love when all is good, but what happens when you're tired, when you're hurt, when you're angry? Love is what keeps you from building a wall and keeps you grounded.

So, how do you love God? In John 13, 14, and 15, God tells us, if we love Him, we will keep His commandments. To love God is to show Him obedience.

The second fruit is joy. Joy is something that comes into our hearts. It is a result, a bi-product of walking with the Lord. It comes when you have unity of the Spirit with God. It is displayed multiple times in the Old Testament as an emotion.

In the New Testament, it is stated multiple times "for you joy to be complete." Which tells us that it does require something to be fulfilled. Even though it is invisible, it has visible expressions. Many feel joy is just having a peaceful soul. It is portrayed as a calm, serene feeling, but it's more than that. David dances in joy, making a fool of himself to glorify God. John 15 says, "If you obey my commandments you will remain in my love. I have told you this that my joy may be in you." When you seek God's will, there is no shortage of joy, and it will overwhelm you in times of trials, blessings, and dryness. Many will confuse gratification with joy. Gratification of giving into the flesh is a temporary fulfillment that cannot remain.

The third is peace. This fruit is difficult. We are good at faking it, at portraying the image of being a calm, collected family. This fruit is one we must fight for. "Peace" is a loaded word. It refers to mental, emotional, and physical peace, as well as peace in our relationships with each other. Jesus is the Prince of Peace. Peace is the state of heaven. It is a common misconception that peace simply means there is no fighting. Anyone who is married knows that is far from the truth. Peace is the ability to address the hostility between two parties to reach an agreement.

For followers of Christ, this can be a struggle. We go to church, we greet one another, we fake peace, yet we are angry with God, or feel distant, or frustrated. The church often makes us feel that these sentiments are not allowed, but they are human. When we avoid God, we ignore the Spirit convicting us, we suppress the anger or lost feeling when something dramatic happens, we pretend the issue we are dealing with is none of God's business. By doing that, we are faking peace, not living in it. Moreover, we are actually committing an act hostile toward God. In Romans 8, it says the mind is hostile toward God. Until we confront these emotions and come to God vulnerable and bare, we cannot achieve peace in our souls.

The other side is to tell God, "You do your thing, and I'll do mine." It's the polar opposite and still leaves us without peace. Ephesians 2:14 states, "For he himself is our peace, who has made us both one and has broken down in his flesh the dividing wall of hostility." Jesus came to spate the wall that kept us from God, but he also came to break the wall of hostility between each other.

The fourth fruit is patience. The Greek word for patience means "slow to anger." This is the character for God. Throughout all of Scripture, you hear God is slow to anger. In fact, the reason God hasn't returned is because he is patiently waiting for more people to find him. Matthew 18:21-35 is a parable of the unforgiving servant. It says, "Then Peter came up and said to him, 'Lord, how often will my brother sin against me, and I forgive him? As many as seven times?' Jesus said to him, 'I do not say to you seven times, but seventy-seven times.'"

Therefore, the kingdom of heaven may be compared to a king who wished to settle accounts with his servants. When he began to settle, one was brought to him who owed him ten thousand talents. Since he could not pay, his master ordered him to be sold, with his wife and

Fingerprint Series 39

children and all that he had, and payment to be made. The servant fell on his knees, imploring him, "Have patience with me, and I will pay you everything." Out of pity for him, the master of that servant released him and forgave him the debt.

But, when that same servant went out, he found one of his fellow servants who owed him a hundred denarii, and, seizing him, he began to choke him, saying, "Pay what you owe." So his fellow servant fell down and pleaded with him, "Have patience with me, and I will pay you." He refused and put him in prison until he could pay the debt. When his fellow servants saw what had taken place, they were greatly distressed, and they went and reported to their master all that had taken place.

His master summoned him and said to him, *"You wicked servant! I forgave you all that debt because you pleaded with me. And should not you have had mercy on your fellow servant, as I had mercy on you?"* In anger, his master delivered him to the jailers, until he should pay all his debt. *"So also my heavenly Father will do to every one of you, if you do not forgive your brother from your heart."* Patience and forgiveness go hand and hand. Though they are incredibly difficult it is important we always work on cultivating them, as they are the heart of God.

The fifth fruit is kindness. The meaning of kindness is straightforward, but, in Scripture, you see it paired with its ability to be useful. We all know kindness is doing acts of compassion to those around you. Throughout Scripture, kindness is shown as a disposition toward others to improve their circumstances without an ulterior motive, rather, opening an opportunity for relationship. In our culture today, it is all about networking, and we base so many of our friendships and acquaintances on what we can get out of them. The selfless act of kindness leaves you filled with joy when done with the right heart, and is God's intent.

Next is goodness. How do you even begin to explain God's goodness? How is it different than kindness? This concept confused me. "Good" is such a generic term that is interchanged with kindness so much that the differences are subtle. We grow up understanding what is good and bad by culture. In the Bible, it explains that a good deed is something done in alignment with God's standards and holiness. We understand this by renewing our minds. This is seen in Romans 12: 2, "Do not be conformed to this world,[c]but be transformed by the renewal of your mind, that by testing you may discern what is the will of God, what is good and acceptable and perfect."

The seventh fruit is faithfulness. This fruit is one that is a constant battle for many Christians. I am so thankful that God is faithful. He says no one can take us from His hand. He is the same yesterday, today, and tomorrow. His love for us is unmatched and unwavering. We need to work this quality into ourselves to be faithful to each other, but also to God. How often do we find ourselves easily distracted, too tired for church, or wanting to watch TV until we fall asleep and forget to pray? The enemy wants be there in your lax of faithfulness and for you to be in a comfort zone where you slowly begin to lose sight of your relationship with God and others. Deuteronomy 7:9 says, "Know therefore that the LORD your God, He is God, the faithful God, who keeps His covenant and His lovingkindness to a thousand generation with those who love Him and keep His commandments."

Last is self-control. This topic is a book in itself. One I could not write. I look at such simple things as follow-through, and I get so sidetracked or tired, I forget to follow up. It's not hard, just time-consuming. That's the problem with today. Want to lose weight? Just diet and go to the gym. How many people make a New Year's resolution, only to break it a few weeks later? Why? Because we have no self-control.

Proverbs 16:32 says, "Whoever is slow to anger is better than the mighty, and he who rules his spirit than he who takes a city." What this is saying is we can make better judgements when we are able to take our emotions out of the picture and think rationally. To control our own desires, it takes constant management. To identify, improve, and stretch ourselves takes a lot of work. It is uncomfortable and frustrating, but, when we achieve it for a particular moment, the results are incredible in the wisdom we receive.

DAILY INSPIRATIONS

- *Fruit is expected*
- *Fruit can be inspected*
- *Fruit cannot be manufactured*

REFLECTIONS

Do you see God producing fruit in your life?

Do you produce fruit by your own actions or God's opportunity?

What fruit do you feel God has gifted you with?

Fingerprint Series

CHAPTER SIX

Prayer

We always hear about how important prayer is, yet it can feel difficult. I have been a believer my whole life, so talking to thin air isn't as foreign to me as it is to others. Even though I have prayed routinely since I was a child, I still have a hard time. The thing is prayer is such a powerful tool, it is the lifeline to our relationship. It gives peace in fear, it brings joy to brokenness, and it restores hope when you feel lost. All of this comes from some quiet time with God. Why, then, is it so hard?

To understand why prayer is so difficult, let's look at how you pray. Some people pray in the car, some on a walk, and some in bed at night. When you pray matters, but how you pray makes all the difference. Ask yourself these questions: Do your prayers thank God? Do your prayer ask God more than thank Him? Do you have a checklist of what to ask God when you pray?

These questions are a glimpse of what you are seeking in your heart. The posture of your heart is how you will feel in prayer. I am as guilty of it as the next person. When I pray, I often begin to make it about me and my checklist of what I need and want in my life. Before I know it, I am fitting God into my preplanned life, again forgetting that He is in control and already has a plan for my life. When I find myself in that mode, prayer becomes distant, difficult, and dry. I feel like I'm talking to no one. That I'm alone and, honestly, crazy. I get frustrated, mad, and often overwhelmed. That will happen. I get frustrated with people who make their prayer life sound so much more wonderful than mine. Just because their prayer life is great at that moment doesn't mean it's always that way. But why doesn't anyone ever talk about when you feel abandoned? How do we get back to hearing God?

First, change your view of prayer. If you are feeling distant, it is most likely because you are asking for a checklist of wants from God. When you do that, you are seeking your goals, but that may not be in alignment with God. If it is not, you will be frustrated for a long time. At least, until you give that up and start praying a different way. Begin to pray for God to show you the opportunity in the situation. If it is a job, ask for the right one to make the offer. If it is a particular situation or health, ask for God to reveal the purpose. Every trial, every joy that is placed in our life has an opportunity to be used *by* God *for* God. We need to refocus ourselves to see what that is.

Second, it is important to rethink how you pray. So often, we go to God, and we start to question Him. "God, why didn't I get that job?" "If you can just help me find a boyfriend/girlfriend, Lord." "God, if you could just..." We begin to question God either through frustration or through doubt. Both leave a self-centeredness that blocks you from hearing Him. Sometimes I hear Him and don't like the answer, so I ignore it.

For prayer to be effective, you must understand the power of spiritual warfare. The devil will have you believe you are helpless, worthless, and incapable of taking control of your life. The truth is we have had authority instilled in us that Satan is not capable of touching us. When we pray in the authority of God, standing on his promises, pleading the blood, we are untouchable, and unstoppable. In the chapter on trials, we will examine this closer to understand how the authority given to us impacts the spiritual realm.

Pray in the power of God's promises. There are multiple verses to stand on, but, rather than list them, below is a prayer I have used when I needed to feel God there. Here's the secret, though. You'll start praying just to pray. That isn't enough. When you are feeling lost, alone, or frustrated, it's like the final quarter of the homecoming game. You're down by a touchdown, and your team is five yards from the endzone. Would you just calmly say, "Go team"? Absolutely not! You would be standing screaming, "Let's go, boys. You got this! LET'S GO, TEAM!"

Prayer is no different. When you're in that moment with God, be all in! Get on your knees, say the promises with conviction, free from doubt. With conviction, you know he's listening. Have conviction that the enemy cannot touch you. Conviction that God will be there for you. Conviction that God is holding you. Conviction that tomorrow, when you wake up, it will be different. God will show you the reason; He'll bring back the joy, He will restore peace, and He will give grace and hope to continue the march forward in whatever season you are going through. I hope this prayer helps you stand in whatever moment you are at.

> "God, I don't know what to do right now, but I know that you are in control. I know that you promised never to leave me (Hebrews 13:5). I don't know why this is happening and I want so badly to please you. God, you promised you would be there for me. You are my foundation, my rock (Psalm 18:2). You promised to give me strength when I am tired (Isaiah 40:29). You promised that all things will work for good (Romans 8:28) and, although I don't understand this, Lord, I pray it can be used to glorify you. God, I know that the enemy wants to tear me down. To make me fail and hurt my relationship with you. But I know that he has no authority here. That your word will always prevail, and your will will be done (Isaiah 55:10-11). God, I thank you that you are the same every day, that you are faithful (1 Thessalonians 5:24) and will always provide for me (Philippians 4:19). God, you promised never to give me more than I can handle (1 Corinthians 10:13), and I pray you show me your will in this. I pray this in the name of Jesus. Amen.

You don't have to quote scripture word-for-word. As long as you know the promises and pray in the authority and plead the blood, Satan *cannot* touch you.

Third, pray for God's glory. When you are praying for God's will and not your own, you'll begin to see a bigger picture. Last, pray with a thankful heart. The posture of our heart is everything. Philippians 4:12 says, "I know what it is to be in need, and I know what it is to have plenty. I have learned the secret of being content in any and every situation, whether well fed or hungry, whether living in plenty or in want." If we want to take control of our life from the enemy, we must work on this verse. We are not guaranteed an easy life, but, if we are able to see God work it for good, we can be thankful.

C.S. Lewis said, "We ought to give thanks for all fortune; if it is 'good,' because it is good, if 'bad', because it works in us patience, humility, and the contempt of this world and the hope of our eternal country." When we go through something bad, it helps us to grow in maturity and faith. This is so important, but C.S. Lewis brought up another interesting concept to add to this. In his book *The Screwtape Letters*, he talks about the posture of prayer. The posture of our heart is key, but what can help put us in that place is our physical posture. When we pray on our knees, it shows humility; it shows respect (and it helps keep you from falling asleep). In the book, it talks about how if we do not take the posture of prayer seriously, we do not take the prayer as seriously. Personally, it has impacted me to consider where my heart is. Am I still, undistracted, and humbled? Or am I just checking my faith off my to-do list? I'll let you decide.

Pray knowing this: Satan is afraid of our prayers. The power it holds: such as healing, speaking in tongues, and visions give us hope, joy, peace, and authority he cannot control. One reason is because your prayers can change circumstances in the spiritual realm (which we'll talk about next chapter). This means you give angels fuel to fight and can help change a situation. James 5:16-17 states, "Therefore, confess your sins to one another and pray for one another, that you may be healed. The prayer of a righteous person has great power as it is working. Elijah was a man with a nature like ours, and he prayed fervently that it might not rain, and for three years and six months it did not rain on the earth."

Second, prayer has the power to affect someone else's life. When you pray over someone, or for someone, you are fighting for them. This can change Satan's whole plan when, for instance, someone is healed after being prayed over. Prayer is so crucial, but it can become so routine, even for me! Keep reminding yourself of the power it holds and how it will change everything.

FOOD FOR THOUGHT

- *Pray for God's Will, God's Glory, and stand in his promises*
- *Satan cannot touch you when you plead the blood*
- *Satan is afraid of our prayer*

REFLECTION

What are your prayers centered on?

Has your perspective of prayer changed?

What can you pray for to help fight in the spiritual realm?

Fingerprint Series

CHAPTER SEVEN

How to Control Our Demons

If you're anything like me, you may feel you have spent your whole life on the spiritual battleground. I was constantly fighting for my faith in my life, but, for me, it hit the hardest in high school. Those years are when you begin to start challenging your faith. Do I go to church just because my parents say so? Do I want to fit in? Can cussing and sex be that bad? Suddenly, you're questioning yourself and your faith. This is where so many get lost. They will be so desperate to create themselves a certain image, that they will lose who they truly are. To understand how to fight a battle, you cannot see that you must understand what you are fighting.

Now, I'm about to begin down a path that many will call taboo. Many will call this section controversial. You may take of it what you will, but I say this out of experience. Not only my own, but my husband's, and my family's. I believe and have experienced the games and tactics used to try and manipulate my life. I have seen the effects of both winning and losing these battles. You will not always win, but you can affect how much they will impact you.

Fear and intimidation are the game of Satan, but what he doesn't want you to realize is that he cannot touch you without God's consent.

How do you begin to protect yourself against Satan? You must start by building a stronghold in your mind. There are two different ways you will be attacked. Spiritually, which is to question God or keep you from a relationship with Him. Then, there is the mental attack, in which insecurities, jealousy, and character flaws begin to take hold of you, so you don't reach your potential.

Satan attacks both ways, in an attempt to make you seem distant from God or unworthy. The goal is to take you from thinking about God altogether and get you going sideways. In these moments, you feel so alone, that you do not feel you can overcome the mountain in front of you. No matter what illusion Satan plays, there is nothing that can separate you from the love of God. You must learn to recognize what you are fighting before you begin. Otherwise, you become emotionally charged, focused on fighting with feeling verses logic, and lose sight of what is important.

Ephesians 6:12 says, "For our struggle is not against flesh and blood, but against the rulers, against the authorities, against the powers of this dark world and against the spiritual forces of evil in the heavenly realms." If you have not read *The Screwtape Letters* by C.S. Lewis, DO IT! I'm always on the run, so I listen to a lot of audiobooks. This book goes by quickly when you're driving around listening. It's about four hours long, and it will open your eyes to many ways we are manipulated by the enemy.

Among other lessons, Lewis discusses how the road to hell is a slow and gradual one, with no sudden jerks or twists. A life without attacks is a house of faith built of straw. Don't let the temporary satisfaction keep you from seeing truth: God is the only thing that can satisfy us.

God gives us spiritual weapons to fight Satan. Ephesians 6:10-18 states, "Finally, be strong in the Lord and in the strength of his might. Put on the whole armor of God, that you may be able to stand against the schemes of the devil. For we do not wrestle against flesh and blood, but against the rulers, against the authorities, against the cosmic powers over this present darkness, against the spiritual forces of evil in the heavenly places. Therefore take up the whole armor of God, that you may be able to withstand in the evil day, and having done all, to stand firm. Stand therefore, having fastened on the belt of truth, and having put on the breastplate of righteousness, and, as shoes for your feet, having put on the readiness given by the gospel of peace. In all circumstances take up the shield of faith, with which you can extinguish all the flaming darts of the evil one; and take the helmet of salvation, and the sword of the Spirit, which is the word of God, praying at all times in the Spirit, with all prayer and supplication. To that end, keep alert with all perseverance, making supplication for all the saints." There is so much packed into this scripture, and, although it is pretty straightforward, if you have not done a study on it, I would encourage you to delve further into this verse.

When I was in high school, I really started to struggle when I began to understand I could either fit in or follow God. There is not an option to do both. I became very guarded, to the point I judged everyone around me to help me feel safer and help me feel better about being alone. In high school, I had a bad experience with a small group in church that caused me to leave for a few years. I still listened to sermons online, but couldn't go to one more place I felt so alone.

I began to get picked on. What I didn't realize at the time, was those kids who tried to bully me were dealing with their own insecurities. They were incapable of feeling okay with themselves, so they had to tear down someone else to make themselves feel good. This began those little voices in my head that say "you're nothing," "you can't do it," "don't you wish you could be like them?" These are just the enemy trying to destroy what you were created to be in Christ. If you want a great book, read *The Bait of Satan* by John Bevere. It is an in-depth book, addressing attacks like pain from being hurt or offended by an experience, and it has provides a step-by-step process to fight Satan in the Spiritual Realm and build a stronghold in Christ.

You are unique, quirky, and awkward at times, and that's okay. You can feel so alone when you can't find anyone to relate to. You may look at the big group of friends others have and be jealous; you want that. I was a cheerleader, so I was pretty well-known, but I never fit in. I sat by myself on the bus to and from games. The other girls wouldn't talk to me; they considered me boring and naïve, because I wasn't having sex or going to parties. Some even spread rumors about me, and I wanted to break.

There were days—actually, most days— I went home crying. I thought, "I'll just sleep with someone. I'll just go get drunk one time, and that will fix it." No matter how much I wanted to, the Holy Spirit was always there saying, "Do you want to compromise who you are for them? Are they worth losing yourself over? Do you think that will make them care?" And I am so grateful for that. I could have let it all go. I could have become just like everyone else, but I didn't. The love of God never left me, and, because of the Holy Spirit, God was always there whispering that I was loved, that I was meant for more.

The challenges I faced in high school were just the beginning, and they prepared me for much larger mountains I would have to climb. I had to realize my fight was not against people; it was against Satan. He had found a new foothold on me, and I had to break it. First, his foothold was the desire for acceptance. Next, it was through my ex-boyfriend. Now, it is through family. Once you recognize the attack, it becomes much easier to manage it. You realize what you are fighting, then, you battle. The best part is: you don't do it alone. In the next chapter, we'll talk about how to battle, but, for now, let's stay focused on *how* the attacks come. They are constantly shifting.

From a young age, Satan will first attack your confidence. He will do anything to get you to focus on yourself, rather than on God. God will shape you and grow you, you do not have to worry about it. But, if you are distant from God, Satan can begin working on your soul. Which means working to destroy your mind, will, and emotions. This will become extremely evident when you fall: sleeping around, drinking, doing drugs, and acting in ways other than those God wants for you. Satan will make you feel you are not good enough. You failed and are not worthy; you should be ashamed; you deserve to be punished and suffer. In these times, remember Peter's story. God is ready to forgive those who ask with a sincere heart.

Then, it becomes more complicated. The first goal of Satan is to distract you, so you cannot feel the Holy Spirit. If he succeeds in that, the rest is easy; they can manipulate your soul. It starts small, with something as simple as making you judgmental of the church. As I said earlier, I had a bad experience and know how difficult church is sometimes, but churchgoers are just people, like you and me, and there is still a lot of good that comes from church. People are broken, but God is not. If nothing else, go for the sermon. You must hear the word of God for it to be active in your life! The demon will taunt you with your faith. You'll begin to have thoughts like::

- This music is too old, loud, slow, fast…etc.
- These people are too friendly/ not friendly enough.
- I can't stand "church" people.
- I can't be real around "church" people.

The only time I encourage considering a new church is when you don't feel yourself growing. If you can leave every week and not think about what was said or feel you need to work on something… it's time to find something that encourages your relationship with God. Being challenged is good, and a necessary part of life.

Satan is a master of making you feel uncomfortable in your own skin. Thinking you can't or won't fit in, when no one feels like they fit in! If you stop hearing the Word and having it stirred up in your heart, you become complacent. You begin to miss prayer here and there. Then, you promise yourself you'll get back to it…but this weekend I have (fill in the blank). Next thing you know, it's been a few months, and you haven't been to church. You haven't spent time with God. And you're happy; you're doing fine. It only when the attack or trial hits that all of a sudden, we go back to our roots. We begin to pray diligently, and remember we need God.

Sometimes, this doesn't happen for years. In *God's Not Dead*, watch the scene with the mother and son. It's a quick clip that you can find on YouTube. Go ahead…go search for it!

In the scene, a son goes to see his mother, who has dementia. He states that she was such a wonderful person and look at what she got, yet he is the meanest, and his life is perfect. How do you explain that? The mother responds that life can be like a jail cell, and Satan will make it full of luxury to keep you from walking out. Before you realize it, the door slams shut, and it's too late. Many will dismiss it and say it's just a movie, but it's not. Listen to the words, and take note of them.

Satan will continue to work on destroying your soul. Things like greed, pride, and power begin to consume you. You need to do more, be more, get more. You begin to consider yourself better than others, which can cause bitterness through thoughts like, "I deserved that promotion more. I deserve a raise, because I've been here two years." Before you know it, you are consumed with getting yourself to the next level you desire, instead of focusing on what God has and the opportunity He set up for you!

Today's culture forces bitterness and unrest on us through marketing images that bombard us wherever we turn. We see the cars, watches, and lifestyles we crave. But the secret to success is not focusing on the things you don't have. The secret is to constantly work on yourself as God uses trials to help you grow. As this happens, so will your opportunities. I'm not saying don't have a goal. Rather, to achieve your goal, you cannot focus solely on the end, you must see the path and plan your steps. This is *hard* work, and it requires dedication and self-discipline. That is why so many will not make it.

Let's clarify something about God and Satan. God will give you trials. Trials are tests designed to bring you closer to Him and shape you into Christ's likeness. Attacks from Satan, on the other hand, are designed to hurt you. God, like a parent, will give trials out of love. However, in these trials, He is always with us. His love guides, and, in His promises, he has stated he will never give us more than we can handle. I'm not a fan of that saying, though. I personally feel that God gives us *just* more than we can handle, so that we surrender and admit we need him. Satan's attacks are designed to steal, kill, and destroy. All Satan wants is to steal your joy and happiness, kill your self-worth, and destroy your legacy. Every marriage, every bond between a parent and child, every action of good intent, he will work to twist and make miserable.

To handle the attacks that are coming, we must know that God is always with us, that His love and power overcomes all. Start this by accepting your weaknesses, and know they will be used against you. Learn to recognize them.

I have struggled with this, myself. When my husband and I were dating, I wanted to find his faults. Thoughts like, *He hasn't taken me on a spontaneous date in a while, so he must not love me as much,* began plaguing me. This could not be further from the truth! Then, we got married, and things changed. *Why doesn't he clean without me asking? He hasn't brought home flowers in a while, so he must not care.* And the biggest one I've had to struggle with is his car. I became very jealous of how much he loved that car (for other wives, it may be sports) and wanted to war over the car. Until I realized how silly I was being.

Now, it's my own family. In the past year, I recognized the attack on my husband had moved on to my family. Satan knows how to deliver an uppercut. I didn't see it coming. It crippled me. I stopped talking to my dad for a month, and I fought with my brother multiple times. I've always been the problem -olver of the family, and, when I felt abandoned by my family— which was one of Satan's manipulation tactics— I got angry. As my brother and mom began to fight, I wanted to protect each of them, and I, too, began to fight. In that moment, I had to decide what I was fighting for.

I also had a child this year, which was another major mental battle. Baby blues are real, but you must prepare to fight. The truth is you control how you feel, you just have to take the time to step back and rationalize it. This is difficult at first. There are still times I get emotionally charged and can't think straight. Sometimes, I just want to be angry, and that's fine. Take a run, or go for a walk. You just have to remove yourself from doing something you will regret. An indicator I learn to look for is when I start to lose control and don't know why; that is when you're being attacked. When you lash out at work, because you're irritated for no reason, or when you snap at your partner, because you're taking it the wrong way, even when you know that's not what was meant. When you're looking for the negative in someone or going after them, that is the moment you get to decide to press into God and give Him control, or give in and let Satan manipulate you.

If you have seen the movie *War Room,* there is the moment she decides to fight, to acknowledge God's power, and to realize He is in control. Through prayer and standing in God's promises in the Scripture, she takes control of the situation by surrendering to God. It is a funny but powerful scene and, often, the power of prayer is downplayed. Prayer is a lifeline that gives God control, the Holy Spirit a strong voice, and the Scripture authority in our lives.

To fight the Spiritual Realm, you must understand it. So, let's go back to the basics of the Spiritual Realm. There are angels, and there are demons. When Satan turned against God, he was cast out of Heaven. At that time, one-third of the angels decided to follow him. When they came down to Earth, they became "fallen angels," also known as demons. This is seen in Revelation 12:4. The Bible doesn't use this term, but it is the common reference to describe these supernatural beings. Satan has control of these "fallen angels," and he uses them to attack us. These beings are evil, and in Jude 1:6, they are described as being kept in eternal chains, awaiting God's judgement when Christ returns. These demons have one goal: to deceive you and make you feel separated from God.

Angels, on the other hand, are often thought of as little, glowing, timid beings who are there to whisper sweet things on your shoulder. That could not be further from the truth. If you read 2 Kings, you will adjust your thoughts, I guarantee! In this scene, an army is coming to kill Elisha. His servant is panicked, warning him they need to leave.

In 2 Kings 6:17, it says, "And Elisha prayed, 'Open his eyes, LORD, so that he may see.' Then the LORD opened the servant's eyes, and he looked and saw the hills full of horses and chariots of fire all around Elisha." What the assistant was seeing was the spiritual realm. He sees angels in chariots of fire and horses. These angels are warriors, designed to help and protect us. In Revelation, it talks about the "final battle". Revelation 20:7-10 says," And when the thousand years are ended, Satan will be released from his prison and will come out to deceive the nations that are at the four corners of the earth, Gog and Magog, to gather them for battle; their number is like the sand of the sea. And they marched up over the broad plain of the earth and surrounded the camp of the saints and the beloved city, but fire came down from heaven and consumed them, and the devil who had deceived them was thrown into the lake of fire and sulfur where the beast and the false prophet were, and they will be tormented day and night forever and ever." There isn't even a fight. God just shows up, and that's it! These angels are not shy, timid, scared creatures. They are strong, powerful, and equipped to help you.

There is a hierarchy of how the spiritual realm works. The structure is simple. God is above all. Then, there is us! We are above all else. Then, Satan, angels, and demons are below us. You may wonder why we have authority. If you look at the Latin word Imago Dei, it means "image of God." We have one thing no other creation has, including angels. We were designed to be like God, and, with that, we also have his authority. In Genesis 1:27, it states, "God created man in his own image." This gives us the unique ability to reflect God intellectually and spiritually. Understand that God instilled His spirit in you and gave you authority, just as a boss does to a manger.

Many people think Satan and God are on an equal level. It is the greatest deception Satan can give us, other than making the world think he doesn't exist. However, when you read Revelation, you will find God doesn't rush to the battlefield to take on Satan. Instead, he sends Michael, the Archangel, and simply destroys Satan's army with fire. We tend to minimize God and make Satan huge, thinking we cannot overcome the battle, but we already have!

Let's break it down to summarize. God is the creator and has created everything, which means all things were created "by him, for him." When God sent his son, Jesus, to come die for our sins, John 3:16, Jesus took full authority of the Earth. Colossians 2:15 says, "(Jesus) disarmed the rulers and authorities[a] and put them to open shame, by triumphing over them in him." God is in control, and Jesus has the authority— the same authority he gives to us through the Holy Spirit. Because we are designed by him, for him, he has promised us to love and protect us. In Hebrews 13:5-6, He, Himself, said, ""I will never desert you, nor will I ever forsake you," so that we confidently say, "The Lord is my helper, and I will not be afraid." Knowing Jesus came and conquered this world, we can rest in the fact that he has conquered every attack and has already won our battle. To help us in the attacks, we can use spiritual weapons

DAILY INSPIRATIONS

- *Our battle is against Satan not others*
- *Satan will focus on attacking spiritually and mentally*
- *God gives trials for growth*
- *Satan does attacks to steal, kill, and destroy*

REFLECTIONS

Can you see an attack in your life currently?

What is usually your first reaction in an attack?

What is your favorite verse to stand on when you are in a trial?

Fingerprint Series

CHAPTER EIGHT

How to Prepare for the Trials What They Produce

Satan attacks, but God gives us trials. We must be able to recognize the two. In either situation, you can always stand on the promises of God. Understanding Scripture, God's love, and how the Holy Spirit lives in you is vital to being a believer and staying faithful to God. Satan will try and twist scripture. He will try to use it against you, just like he did Eve in the garden and even Jesus in the desert. He cannot manipulate what you know, though. That is another reason it is important to be listening to the Word. To become mentally strong is to rest in these promises and keep hope. It's funny how if you're watching a sports game, players will give you their best if they have hope. When it's a close game, the teams battle, giving their blood, sweat, and tears to try and gain the upper hand. The best is when there is that large gap in the score, and you've counted the other team out, and, in the final stretch of the seventh inning, the bases get loaded, and you can feel the anticipation in the air. The excitement builds as the chants start and the batter walks to the plate. You're just praying he doesn't strike out, and holding your breath as he gets a strike. Next thing you know, it's a hit, and it's dead silent as the crowd waits to see if it's fair or foul. Right as it goes over the stands, it's a home run, and the crowd erupts. Everyone is on their feet, and the entire mood changes. Suddenly, there is hope to pull through, even though you're still down.

It is the same in our spiritual battle. The only difference is we're the guy at bat. No pressure, right! Through his final curve balls, change-ups, and sliders, Satan is trying to make you feel discouraged. You may strike out, but you could swing for the fences, too! The power of hope makes you unstoppable.

Sometimes, we need the darkness to see the light. Trials show you how real your faith is. Like the stars, they shine and guide not only you, but those around you. In your trials, you set an example for God. When you can display peace, calm, and joy while others tell you you're nothing, you can't make it, or you've lost… that is when God shines through.

The beauty of trials is they are for a purpose and done with love. Usually, it is to bring you back to God, work out a bad quality you've created, or build up a gift God has given you. If you read the story of Joseph in Genesis, he was sold into slavery by his brothers. Then, he was falsely accused of trying to sleep with his master's wife and placed in jail. He did not deserve any of this; however, it led to him being the leader of Egypt and saving a nation. There is a small part of the story though that took me back, when Joseph was in jail had interpreted two dreams and asked the cupbearer of the king to remember him. Joseph had self-pity. Satan still had a stronghold on him for what he was going through, and, because of that, God could not bring him out of his trial just yet. Two years later, Joseph was brought out of jail and placed as head of Egypt, saving the entire nation from famine. When his brothers come to him, he did not have hatred, or anger. Rather, he had love. Joseph did, however, still made his brothers sweat a little. I appreciate the human aspect of this part of the story. Keeping the mindset of looking at what God is trying to show us will help us exam the trial.

Each trial is allowed by God. Luke 22:31 God says to Peter, "Simon, Simon, behold, Satan has demanded permission to have you, that he might sift you like wheat." And we see with Job, when, again, Satan demands permission to test himThe trials we endure are given to us in portions, but we are always under God's unshakable protection.

God has promised to give us what we can handle…and the escape route! All we need to do is keep our eyes focused on him, and he'll do the rest.

This was hard for me to understand. I am Type A and always have a plan, but God's plan is *not* mine. Many people take this to mean God allows people to be murdered or get cancer. That is not the case. Honestly, I cannot claim to understand our trials, but we must remember an attack is not the will of God. What I had to understand is that God created us with free will. If one person, in their free will, desires to take the life of another, God cannot grant one person free will and the other not. Even the angels can choose if they want to follow God!

When it comes to disease and death, I am no stranger. My grandma died from cancer at sixty-four. My aunt from cancer at forty-five. My grandpa from a stroke at fifty-eight. My cousin lost her baby the week she was due, because of the umbilical cord. I have struggled with why these things happen, and had to accept that one day, I will understand, but that day is not today. It also doesn't stop me from humbling myself and using these experiences to stay grounded. Why stay angry if I could be diagnosed with cancer tomorrow?

Use these situations to teach you the value of what you have. Let God focus on the bigger picture. One day, you will see and know everything you desire, but there is comfort in knowing that God controls it all. One of my favorite quotes is from Reinhold Niebuhr, "God grant me the serenity to accept the things I cannot change, the courage to change the things I can, and the wisdom to know the difference." It doesn't matter how much you stress over a situation, God will answer it in His timing.

To keep the stress at bay, I pray. Spending that moment with Him when I start to feel stress take hold provides peace and reminds me he has overcome this world. Although the trial is here, he reminds me he is carrying me through it. I am never alone. I am loved and cared for by the creator of the universe! I don't know your situation today, but know that God has already conquered it, and he is waiting to hold you.

I envy Paul for his devotion to God and his understanding of this. In Philippians 4:12, he wrote, "I know what it is to be in need, and I know what it is to have plenty. I have learned the secret of being content in any and every situation, whether well fed or hungry, whether living in plenty or in want." Paul constantly worked on himself to build his need in God, and not the world.

C.S. Lewis put a spin on this when he said, "We ought to give thanks for all fortune: if it is 'good,' because it is good, if 'bad' because it works in us patience, humility, and the contempt of this world and the hope of our eternal country." This is not an easy thing to be "worked." I have been pushed to my breaking point many times, and I fall to me knees and beg God to take it from me. That I just can't go one more day, but, then, I get up, and I do. I have met people with cancer who have lived ten years longer than their doctors predicted, and they live each day for God with a vengeance. Christine Cain was diagnosed with throat cancer a few years ago. Satan tried to take her vocal cords, so she could not preach the Word, yet three days after her surgery, she was at the Honda Center in California sharing the message of Christ.

It is not uncommon for Satan to attack in drastic ways once he has lost a stronghold on you in a spiritual way. God is watching, though, and He will use it for good. The following quote by Marc Levy paralyzed me when I first heard it. I hope it helps ground you in whatever moment you're going thorough. "If you want to know the value of one year, just ask a student who failed a course. If you want to know the value of one month, ask a mother who gave birth to a premature baby. If you want to know the value of one day, ask the person who was just diagnosed with cancer. If you want to know the value of one hour, ask the lovers waiting to meet. If you want to know the value of one minute, ask the person who just missed the bus. If you want to know the value of one second, ask the person who just escaped death in a car accident. And if you want to know the value of one-hundredth of a second, ask the athlete who won a silver medal in the Olympics." Time is so precious, to waste it harboring hate, anger, self-pity, or shame is a waste. Don't let Satan take one more second from you.

Fingerprint Series

The greatest gift of being a follower of Christ is that we can rejoice in all situations. This is the third way to walk through a trial. In a trial, we lose that joy and laughter. Do you ever stop to wonder why God created laughter? Remember that God is the creator. He gave us family and friends to help us laugh and find joy as we walk through difficult times. You can choose to spend time and energy worrying, or you can spend it looking for the joy around you. Don't let fear control your mind, just stay focused on the trial that God has already won for you. Know you just need to find His path out. Remember Romans 5:3-5, "And not only this, but we also exult in our tribulations, knowing that tribulation brings about perseverance; and perseverance, proven character; and proven character, hope; and hope does not disappoint, because the love of God has been poured out within our hearts through the Holy Spirit who was given to us."

DAILY INSPIRATIONS

- *Prayer and the Word give hope*
- *Each trial produces good*
- *God promises to guide you through the trail*
- *Don't let Satan steal your time*

REFLECTIONS

Do you feel alone when you are in a difficult time?

What do you do to reach out to God?

Has your life become too fast passed or are you valuing your time?

Fingerprint Series

CHAPTER NINE

Ways to Witness for Christ

If you are a believer, you know how horrifying this chapter can be. For someone who has grown up in faith, I feel like this can come relatively easy, but, to a new believer, the idea of talking about your faith with someone else is terrifying. Everyone has freaked out about this and wondered, *What if I don't know the answer to their questions?* I am here to tell you that that is okay! I am certain there will be questions you don't have the answer to. When I am asked why a horrible thing happened in that person's life, I will openly admit I don't know.

I believe one of the most effective ways to witness is to testify about your faith through your actions and lifestyle. I can tell a believer in a bar, because they're reserved, usually there because of friends, not grinding up on someone looking to go home with them, and not overindulging in their drinks. A person's lifestyle tells you who they are. We have all heard the expression that actions speak louder than words. This is so true. For example, praying before a meal in a restaurant tells people you are a believer.

Titus 2 tells us, "But as for you, teach what accords with sound doctrine. [2] Older men are to be sober-minded, dignified, self-controlled, sound in faith, in love, and in steadfastness. [3] Older women likewise are to be reverent in behavior, not slanderers or slaves to much wine. They are to teach what is good, ⁴ and so train the young women to love their husbands and children, ⁵ to be self-controlled, pure, working at home, kind, and submissive to their own husbands, that the word of God may not be reviled. ⁶ Likewise, urge the younger men to be self-controlled. ⁷ Show yourself in all respects to be a model of good works, and in your teaching show integrity, dignity, ⁸ and sound speech that cannot be condemned, so that an opponent may be put to shame, having nothing evil to say about us. ⁹ Bondservants are to be submissive to their own masters in everything; they are to be well-pleasing, not argumentative,¹⁰ not pilfering, but showing all good faith, so that in everything they may adorn the doctrine of God our Savior.

¹¹ For the grace of God has appeared, bringing salvation for all people,¹² training us to renounce ungodliness and worldly passions, and to live self-controlled, upright, and godly lives in the present age, ¹³ waiting for our blessed hope, the appearing of the glory of our great God and Savior Jesus Christ, ¹⁴ who gave himself for us to redeem us from all lawlessness and to purify for himself a people for his own possession who are zealous for good works."

One of the most amazing things is that we are called to be different from the world. We do not desire and lust after what the world says. We do not hate people; we do not hold a grudge—even when we have the right to; we are at peace, even when we are going through something difficult. This is what we do; it's who we are. It is not by our own will; it is through the Holy Spirit and the immense love of God that we are able to do this. Do not be mistaken, though. When people find out your faith, they watch you, often compare themselves to you, and even justify their lives. That is between them and God. Your responsibility is to be the example.

Many people feel when they need to share their faith, they must be bold speak to many and have all these answers. I personally believe this is an illusion from the enemy to keep us from bringing people to God. We all know the twelve disciples, but do you really? If you have the opportunity, read the book *Twelve Ordinary Men,* by John McArthur. It was a sermon series he turned into a book. It is an easy read that recounts the lives of these twelve men. When you make them human and read about their backgrounds, educations, and personalities, your eyes open up so much!

Earlier, I talked about Peter. Everyone loves Peter. He converted thousands, was outspoken in his faith, and passionate about God. He was the rock God built his church on. In today's world, I look at Greg Laurie, Louie Giglio, Billy Graham, and I think…if only I were like them. Honestly, though, if we were all that way, it wouldn't do God justice.

I like to look at Andrew, Peter's brother, when I talk about witnessing. Andrew was quiet, in the background, and very private. Andrew was the strong, silent type who knew what he believed and didn't need to advertise it, but he still witnessed. He only witnessed one-on-one. Andrew was the type to become your friend and slowly introduce you to God. If he didn't think that would work, he would take you to the person who could witness to you. Andrew was the first disciple. He heard Jesus speak and was ready to follow him, but, before he did, he went home and got Peter. Andrew brought Peter to Jesus. When I look what Peter accomplished because of Andrew's faith, it rocks my world. That is what I thrive on. I may not change the world, but God may use me to change one person's world and use them for another.

There are so many ways you can share your faith, but there are also a few things you should avoid. God has called us to love. For many who grow up in the church, we take a different stance. We end up with holier-than-thou syndrome. I didn't understand this when I was younger. I was guarded against those I knew were different than me, but I didn't understand the grace of God. I was very judgmental and closed-minded, and I had no problem telling others when I thought they were doing something wrong.

If you do a study of 1 Corinthians, you will read very clearly what Paul thinks about this. You see, we are to judge to an extent, but it is reserved for those in the church. I say this with caution, because that does not mean you walk up and shame a person, but it does mean if you see someone living outside the will of God, we are required to let them know *lovingly.*

In today's world, the trend is to live together without getting married. When that happens, I challenge my friends and say, "You believe in God, you want to serve God, and you want God to bless your home. How can God bless you, if you are deliberately disobeying his commandments?" It is not condemning, it is not shaming, it is simply asking questions for them to consider the effects of what they do. I am no master at this, and, sometimes, it has gone horribly wrong, but I must try.

For those who live outside of faith, we are not to condemn, but to love them to Christ. This concept has always been difficult for me. To love those outside of faith, to fit in with them to an extent, but not be like them. It is such a fine line that it often doesn't make sense. I go to a bar with a friend, but do not do what they do, I go to a party, but do not drink like they do. I have been judged and told how boring I am for my choices, but I also haven't spent nights with my head in the toilet!

So how do you do this? We must examine your lifestyle. If you are changed by God, you will desire to live a life pleasing to God. Second, you must examine the way you speak. You will notice when a believer talks, they use words like "blessed," instead of lucky. You have control of your tongue. This is *not* easy, but it is possible. The third component is talking about your faith. I openly invite friends to church all the time, and get turned down *all* the time, but it never stops me. When I talk to people, I'll openly say, "I can't that night. I have Bible study." Those small things don't seem like much, but they speak volumes.

I was in a college group with a girl named Kayla, who went to UC Davis. She lived in the dorm and read her Bible every night for a few minutes. One night, she was tired and didn't want to read, but she took out her Bible, anyways. That was the night her roommate asked her why she always reads. That moment opened the door to start a conversation about God. My mom is another example. She grew up very strong in her belief, and she had a few friends in high school she grew apart from. Years later, she received a letter from one friend, telling her how she came to Christ and thanking my mom for her example all those years.

Many people will feel the pressure of need to save a person, but that's not our job. And shoving Jesus down their throat isn't going to change them. We are called to plant the seed. Once they hear what you say, they can't un-hear it. Romans 10:17 says, "So faith comes from hearing, and hearing through the word of Christ." It's a simple concept that we have complicated with rules and concerns.

If you're not a big reader, there is an audiobook called "Share Jesus without Fear," by William Fay. It's an hour long, and it hits all the hotspots. I speaks to our fear of rejection, our fear of not knowing, and our fear of offending them. Fay brings up some incredible points. One of these point is that, of 100 conversions, only 15 percent come to Christ through an event such as Harvest Crusades. 85 percent come from hearing about Jesus 7.6 times before they receive Christ. You may be the third of five times, but each time makes a difference.

It all comes down to this. At the end of the day, you have two choices: You can say something and be used by God, or say nothing and let that person be lost. Even if you say something stupid, incorrect, or unloving, God can use it for God. God can work with our faults to bring a person to Him. What God cannot work with is silence. He has nothing to work with! I would much rather take a chance— and let God do the rest— than sit silently and know God couldn't use me in one of His planned moments for me.

DAILY INSPIRATIONS

- *We are called to be different*
- *We are called to share our faith*
- *We don't have to change the world, just on person's world*
- *God can use anything, but he cannot use silence*

REFLECTIONS

Do you fear anything about sharing your faith?

Do you relate to Peter or Andrew in your witnessing style?

What actions in your life show God?

Fingerprint Series

CHAPTER TEN

Building a Relationship in God with Another

Relationships are complicated, frustrating, and exciting. Cupid and I had a constant struggle with each other, as I constantly fell for the wrong guy, and, if he was the right guy, I was too much of a mess to recognize it. What the mind sees and the heart feel are so far apart, I thought I would be lost in a void of heartbreak forever. The complicated part of playing the game of waiting three days to call, trying not to be too blunt, worrying about why he's not texting me back is that we forget that when we like someone, and they like us, it's just chemistry. This chapter is designed for anyone who desires to expand their view on relationships and grow together with the one they love.

"Love is patient, love is kind. It does not envy, it does not boast, it is not proud. It does not dishonor others, it is not self-seeking, it is not easily angered, it keeps no record of wrongs. Love does not delight in evil but rejoices with the truth. It always protects, always trust, always hopes, always perseveres." 1 Corinthians: 4-7

This quote is one of the most well-known from Scripture. It is a beautiful thought to find someone who can hold all these key qualities; however, it probably won't happen in reality. No matter how hard we try, women will always remember the screw-ups, and men will always exploit their confusion. Dating is complicated and deals with both the good and bad in a person.

What is most important to realize is that love is the greatest gift God can give us. God designed us to crave love. Unfortunately, people mistake love for the satisfaction of having someone praise them. Fulfillment with love does not come by having control over someone. It comes from surrendering everything you have to that person and receiving that back. This is crucial to realize. Many people don't, and then they wind up so starved for attention that they're willing to be in any kind of relationship—even an abusive one), just so they can say, "I have someone." To be able to be in a relationship with someone, you must first be comfortable with you!

There are two things that will destroy a relationship quicker than you can blink.

The first is the lack of satisfaction with yourself. If you are starved for the affection and desire it *too* badly, you will end up driving everyone away. Think of it like the child who always wants a puppy, and, when they do get that puppy, they smother it to death. God created you, and I can assure you he knew what he was doing. Yes, we *all* hate the braces, zits, poorly proportioned body, and, yes, there is always that perfect person you just want to be.

Trust me, I was there, and I was miserable. I was varsity cheerleader, one of the top editors in yearbook, and took multiple AP classes, yet I had no friends and no guy. When the first and only guy in high school asked me on a date my junior year, I wanted the satisfaction of being with somebody so badly I did anything I could to be with him. Let's just say I was a bit obsessed, and, needless to say, it didn't end well.

The problem with self-satisfaction is that it means we expect our partner to provide for our problem. This is something that kills a relationship quickly, because it shows lack of comfort in the relationship. Ladies, if you always have to get dolled up and be told how amazing you look every time, it gets old. No different than when men work out all the time or wear cut off t-shirts, so they can be told how buff they are.

Look, no one is perfect, so don't try to be! You'll be surprised how much that person will love your little quirks, like how girls look in sweats with no makeup, or how a guy can be romantic without fear of being lame.

Japanese philosopher Daisaku Ikeda stated, "In a relationship, it is demeaning to constantly seek your partner's approval. In such relationships, real caring, depth or even love is missing." To have a relationship, one must be comfortable with oneself. We all know that one girl or guy who seems to get anyone they want. I'll bet you they exude confidence and a large attitude. Half the game of high school is confidence, and the rest is not caring, because, trust me, if the "cool" kids cared what people thought, they couldn't keep up with the demands. There is only one you, and, no matter where you go in the world, you will never be like someone else. Everyone has something special to bring to the table, whether it's creativity, romance, or a carefree attitude. The style is yours, so own it!

The second thing that will destroy a relationship is insecurity—also known as ego. Realistically, do we all have them? YES! However, it is important to remember that most of our insecurities come from others' opinions an comments. Honestly, who are they to talk? Insecurities are easily used to manipulate us and, ultimately, cause us to doubt ourselves.

Author Sheri Rose, who wrote the "Love Letters for My Daughter" series, spoke at a tea I attended, and used an analogy that changed my view forever. She spoke of identity theft. We're all familiar with what it means when someone tries to steal your identity and pretends to be you. The worst kind of identity theft, though, is when we allow someone to imprint a behavior or impression on us of who we should be. So often, we neglect to see it's even happening!

In one of my relationships, I was told I was high maintenance, and no one would put up with me. It became a regular thing I was told.

Before I knew it, I wanted more dates, time, and praise. Things like weight, build, and style are so scrutinized that we manipulate ourselves to wear certain clothes or act a certain way to gain acceptance, especially by someone we like.

Let's face it: relationship-wise, our insecurities are huge, because it's new, or an ex destroyed you and tainted your view on what a relationship even is. One of the hardest things to do is control these insecurities and learn to overcome them. I'm here to tell you it can be done…it's just not easy. Girls are known for carrying baggage from their old relationship into a new one. For instance, a form of baggage for both parties is cheating, whether it is emotional or physical cheating. You have two choices: look for the cheater in everyone you date after that, causing a lack of trust, or work hard with the new person to become a great partne,r so they will want to be one, too. The choice is yours.

When it comes to cheating, I have two separate views, depending on the age and the motivation. If you are in high school and this happens, get out! You have so much time, and there are so many options. It is not worth you developing the bad habit that is lack of trust. If you are vested—that is to say if you are engaged or married— I encourage you to look at the motivation behind the cheating. There is absolutely no excuse, but, sometimes, the reason can be rectified. For example, in the movie *Sex and the City*—which is not my favorite example to use but I think a very real portrayal— Miranda Hobbes had an issue with her husband, because she deprioritized him and, after so long of caring about only work and her kid, he couldn't take it anymore. I've heard the saying "once a cheater, always a cheater," but I also don't believe in walking away from a marriage if the reason it stemmed from could be resolved.

So, ladies and gentlemen… if you are with someone who cheated, and you have resolved it, you must leave it resolved. You have two choices: to relive it every moment and let it destroy the relationship slowly, or to let it go and fight to move past it. World-renowned speaker and author Stephen Covey— who is recognized as one of Time magazine's 25 most influential Americans— said, "The most important ingredient we put into any relationship is not what we say or what we do, but what we are." I am not a therapist, but I do know couples who have overcome cheating. The devil is so good at using it to drive you insane, but, if you fight it, if your spouse is doing everything to show you they are willing to fight it, too, it is your choice to fight for it and *through* it to put it in the past and move on.

The main thing about insecurities is we tend to push them onto our partner, and, when we do that, it's like putting an ant under a magnifying glass— eventually, they will burn to death. Insecurities cause a sense of doubt and, ultimately, a lack of trust. A successful relationship must have trust to thrive. Many people build a wall after being hurt and think of the insecurity as a reason to discredit any new person. In reality, the new person didn't do anything to make you not trust them. For example, I had huge insecurities from a cheating situation with my ex, and I had to have a long talk with myself about the reality of it. When I found out my new boyfriend had a female friend, it freaked me out. He worked with her and talked to her a lot. At first, I thought, *Oh, heck no, I'm not doing this again.* I had to remember I have guy friends, and I talk to them a lot, too— I had created a double standard for the two of us. Even worse, I realized he was upfront about his female friend and even took me to his work parties. I cannot even tell you how quickly I wanted to jump on him when I saw a text about them planning to have lunch together. I felt threatened, vulnerable, and uncomfortable with the idea I could be being played again.

I challenge you to reason with yourselves— or, as some people say, choose your battles wisely. Religiously, I warn both guys and girls to use reason, because the enemy is sly. He doesn't pop out and show himself; he attacks through insecurities and doubt. When you see a text that seems "off," fight the doubt. Don't give the devil a chance to toy with you, because he will. You'll be surprised how often you judge someone and go into a situation emotionally loaded, leaving you no choice but to watch your relationship unravel, because, now, your partner feels a lack of trust, and you feel you need to watch them. It's the beginning of the end.

There was one time I found a text on my then boyfriend's phone from a number I didn't know. I opened it, and the girl stated her name and said, "Let's meet tomorrow at lunch." My mind went crazy! I thought, *He's going on a date. He's cheating. How could he?* Instead of freaking out on him right away, I showed him the text and asked him who it was. Turns out it was a girl in his group project coordinating a meeting for everyone. There's no worse feeling than knowing you started a fight over literally nothing and damaged your relationship, just because you couldn't control insecurity.

Gentlemen, it took me many years to scratch the surface of what the male ego consists of, and there's no way to explain it. The best thing I can say is "sensitive." Women have come to accept that you're macho and built tough, but don't hide emotion. Your whole life, you're told suck it up or rub dirt in it, and it's true that as the lead of a relationship or marriage, the man has a certain built-in role to follow. However, if you don't tell the girl what you're thinking, she's built to continue to analyze, probe, and pry until she understands. There is nothing that will hurt a woman more than a lack of emotion. Let's be honest: most of the time you're not sure what you're feeling or how to convey it— and that's fine— but at least tell her that!

The ego of a man and the ego of a boy are very different. A boy's ego is hurt by threatening his title. They tend to need to be the best and prove themselves through sports, games, and girls. A man, on the other hand, is not threatened when you challenge his identity. He knows what he is and accepts it, but his ego kicks in when you challenge his abilities. For instance, most men will have a problem if a girl pays for everything, because he wants to be the provider. A relationship with a man is so much easier, because it is a sense of partnership that we'll talk about later.

The insecurities of a girl and a woman are similar. A girl needs to be reassured a lot and has a tendency to overreact about everything. A woman will overreact to a lack of respect.

WHAT KEEPS US IN A RELATIONSHIP

There is a certain audience reading this book that I hope will take this next part seriously. This is going to sound childish and crazy, but stick with me. I know there are many people who have chosen to stay in a relationship because it's been years, and you are comfortable. I get it. I was deathly afraid to break up with the person I thought was the only stable thing in my life. I believed if I lost him, I would lose it all.

We trick ourselves by remembering the "good times" at the beginning of our relationship. We say things like, "It wasn't always this way," and, "You don't understand the relationship," in order to convince ourselves and our friends that we are okay. You are right; we don't know everything about your relationship. Every week or so, take a piece of paper and write down all the good on one side and all the bad on the other. It may sound lame, but you owe it to yourself to see the outcome. If the good outweighs the bad, awesome!

It wasn't until I started doing this, and seeing week after week the hurt I was enduring, that I was able to let go of my relationship. At the end of the day, staying miserable and comfortable is such an easy option, because to be happy in the unknown seems impossible. To start over and go through the pain of leaving that person seems so much more terrifying then the idea of starting over and finding so much joy. Comfort is a tricky game. However, if you live your whole life in comfort, you would be boring, routine, and predictable. Dwayne "The Rock" Johnson said, "A comfort zone is a beautiful place, but nothing ever grows there."

Part of life is having discomfort and exploring the unknown. Don't let comfort and familiarity become your crutches to give up opportunities that could radically change your life. If you're in that place and walk away and they come back, you know for sure it's right! It's such a cliché, but so true. Then, there are no doubts or mid-life crises when you wake up ten years down the road and say, "I never dated!"

LAYING YOUR FOUNDATION

Before I begin talking about a relationship, let's talk about the hardest part...creating your foundation. This process requires three steps:

1. ***Ensure you are equally yoked.*** I hate discussing this topic for the sole purpose that people love to use it against Christians or any God-following religion. In 2 Corinthians 6: 14, the Bible states, "Do not be yoked together with unbelievers. For what do righteousness and wickedness have in common? Or what fellowship can light have with darkness?" From experience, I can tell you that if you are a believer dating an atheist or even a non-practicing religious person, it's extremely difficult, if not impossible.

   Here's the thing: dating means you will get attached, and, if you chose to go forward with that person, you cannot create a foundation in God and will, ultimately, have huge battles over how to raise your children. You can tell me, "Oh, no, I'll be lenient, and they can raise them however they want," but I'm not buying. There are parents currently suing each other in court to get custody of what religion the child should be! In one of these couples, the mom is Jewish, and the father is Christian. Imagine explaining who Jesus is and, then, explaining that mommy doesn't believe in him! It's confusing to the child, and difficult for both of you. I do believe opposites attract personality-wise, and that is awesome, but to have a strong relationship, you must have the same beliefs.

   Japanese philospher Daisaku Ikeda once said, "Relationships last longer when both partners share similar values and beliefs." In one of my relationships, I was dating a guy who turned twenty-one and thought that bars and parties were the center of life— typical behavior for that age group. However, I'm not a fan of bars and definitely not of being drunk. Parties felt boring and childish. I wanted to stay in and watch movies, play Guitar Hero, or play a round of mini golf...and he wanted to get smashed.

There's no middle ground, and we fought a lot, because he would go out and do it anyway, leaving me at home. Not an ideal relationship. Having the same beliefs is important, because with knowing God comes a joy and peace that not many people have. I can't imagine spending the rest of my life with someone that chooses not to know God, because it breaks my heart that they have no idea what they're missing out on!

2. ***Create a foundation in God.*** Ephesians 2:22 says, "And in him you too are being built together to become a dwelling in which God lives by his Spirit." That sounds confusing, right? It took me twenty years to understand what that meant, and, when I figured it out…I felt a little dumb. To create a foundation in God is to do things to ensure that he is a part of your relationship. This means things like: going to church together, praying together, volunteering at a church together, reading the Bible together, and doing daily devotionals together.

I'm not going to make excuses for anyone, but I do understand what it's like to be busy. When my husband and I were dating, he got a new job that gave him night shifts, and we barely got to see each other. On the weekends, family and church events left us no time. Often, I just wanted to be with him and skip church, but I can testify that a lack of church is the same as lack of oxygen. It's amazing how quickly I become short-tempered and even depressed away from church.

I hated our situation, and, without having God to give both of us peace and joy on Sundays, the situation became bleak. With this difficult schedule, we don't get to do a lot of things together, so church is huge and all we really can do. I email him a daily devotional, and we both read it and email each other a few sentences about it. I love this!

If you're not familiar with a daily devotional, they take about five minutes to read and really change your view throughout the day. We both get energized and often reminded how blessed we are, which restores joy and strength as we go through difficult trials. When you're first starting out, this whole thing may feel awkward and crazy, but, by reading a devotional, praying over meals, and going to church, you will radically see God reach into your relationship and give you joy and blessings I could never describe.

3. ***You must, must, must learn each other.*** In a new relationship, each of you are going to test the boundaries, because you can. Your partner is looking for the line drawn in the sand, so they don't cross it again. When a guy handles a fight by yelling at you, or she cusses at you, or he goes out with other ladies… think of it like a puppy peeing on the nice, white couch in the living room. You must tell them that it's unacceptable.

I have seen many relationships fall apart because someone is trying to be the "cool" boyfriend or girlfriend, and they let things that anger them slide during the first six months or year of the relationship. Suddenly, they wake up, but it's too late to change the relationship.

Remember: iron sharpens iron, and you are improving each other. Not only that, but you are improving the communication with each other. When you establish an effective way of talking to each other, without triggering defensive mode for the other person, your relationship hits a whole new level.

BACK TO THE BASICS

That leads me to a concept that is so simple, yet I know so many relationships that failed because they chose to ignore it. Ready for the big building block in a real mature relationship…communication!

Let me explain something right now: there are girls, and there are women; there are boys, and there are men. Recognizing them is the key to *everything*. Boys and girls will find this next section difficult, if not impossible. These are the typical high school maturity kids who play mind games and have a fear of commitment.

If you are dating and you are serious, read carefully. The foundation of a relationship is built on communication. If you do not establish a way to communicate, you *will* fail in your relationship.

The first key to communication is understanding the hardwiring. Women are built with emotion, which is why we can remember everything. We connect a moment with a song or a scent, and, because of the joy or sadness felt at that moment, we store it forever. The tricky thing about emotion is once something is tied to it, it will not be forgotten.

The best analogy I hear for men and women is that women are spaghetti, and men are waffles. Women are born to multitask. In one fifteen-minute conversation, we can cover work, shoes, vacation, an old memory, food, a movie, and back to shoes…you get the picture. We connect everything! So, ladies, this is a curse and a blessing.

Men, on the other hand, are waffles. They tie few things to emotion and are not designed to scategorize. Men have a certain box for each thing: sports, women, family, school, cars, etc. They can move quickly from one box to another, but the boxes are neatly separated, like the squares of a waffle. This is critical to understand, because men get incredibly frustrated when we jump around to different topics and they can't follow. Usually, women make a poor comment choice and say something like, "Okay, let me slow down for you," or, "What part didn't you get?" Factor in the demeaning tone, and the issues begin! Women: this is so important to remember, so, when you're talking about something big to you (say an upcoming event), stay strictly on that topic, and clearly state what you want.

The second key to communication is use of tone. This is crucial for both sides. Ladies, we are creatures of emotions, which means when we have a bad day, we tend to carry it with us. Be careful: your man is trying to be there for you, so when he looks at you wrong or does something not exactly to par, relax. Never go into a situation loaded

Fingerprint Series

with emotion. When you've had a bad day, remember: he didn't do anything! Even though you ladies are always running on emotion, don't let it get the better of you, especially in heated situations!

Gentlemen, you are creatures of boxes, and you have one box all women despise. It's called the nothing box. How and why men enjoy sitting literally thinking about nothing will always be one of the biggest mysteries to women. Men, be warned: this box leads you into trouble without fail!

Commonly, when a guy is in the nothing box, he forgets when to tune back in. For instance, when your girlfriend spent two hours getting ready and she asks you how she looks and you say "great" in a flat tone…game over. Girls are designed to analyze, and we *can* and *will* analyze every look in your eye and the tone of every word. Men, we understand your love to focus on nothing and I daresay envy it, but, when your lady is around…focus!

Mastering these two building blocks of communication is not too difficult. The one that might cause struggle is changing how you convey things. Ladies, there is one thing I have learned, and if you get nothing else out of this book learn this! If you have a problem with something and you start off the conversation with something like, "I can't believe you just said that," or, "You're such a jerk," your man will *instantly* put up the wall of defense, tune you out, and think of everything and the kitchen sink to throw at you. Every human is built with a comfort line. We accept things easily if there a compliment or shallow criticisms, but everyone has a certain point at which they put up a defense and become unreceptive to anything anyone is saying.

For instance, it's easy for me to hear I'm Type A, but I become defensive when people tell me I'm a control freak. The solution is easy, but you must remember it, even when emotions are running high. They're called "I statements." Our first instinct for both guys and girls is to use you statements. We're all guilty of using them to point the finger. This is where girls pull out everything you've done wrong and guys dig up anything that bothers them.

Instead of saying things like, "I can't believe you ____," it is important to present your concern in a manner that your partner will be receptive to. To bypass that defense line and get your partner to see where you're coming from, reframe what you are saying by using statements like, "It really hurt me when ____," or, "Can you explain what you meant by that, because I took it to mean ____," or, "Next time, can you say it this way, so it doesn't hurt me or make me feel ____." Sounds so simple, right? But add emotion when you're hurt, and it won't be the first thing you want to say. I can promise you that adjusting these tiny statements will change your entire relationship and help with the next part…anger.

"In your anger do not sin. Do not let the sun go down while you are still angry, and do not give the devil a foothold" Ephesians 4:26-27

Men, God wrote this verse for a reason… to protect you! Women analyze, and what that means is that as you sleep—because the issue wasn't such a big deal to you—women lie in bed, analyzing the situation and making it bigger. By the time morning comes…well, think of it like the theme song from Jaws. It starts with a slow *da da*, and, by morning, her mind is going *dadadadadadada,* until she sees you and wants to bite your head off! In a fight, there will be times where you want to get out. Trust me when I say if you leave a fight, it only makes the situation bigger.

Ladies, there are two things to keep in mind. First, we have this lovely habit that when our adrenaline starts flowing, we talk faster. Since your man is not made to Scatagorize, this usually means when you finish your long speech, he'll look at you and say "Huh?" Of course, this makes us even angrier. Per the request of all men, slow down when you're your mad! It is necessary to stay calm and talk the situation out.

Second, for anyone who hasn't seen *The Emperor's New Groove*, I highly recommend renting it. Watch the character Cronk, and notice his obliviousness to Esma's anger. This is a perfect depiction men in a fight. When men sense a fight, testosterone begins to build. Let's face it: when men have a surge of hormones flowing through

Fingerprint Series

their body, they're not known for making smart choices. In a fight, just remember to use I statements, and immediately address what triggered you. In the beginning of a relationship, this will happen a lot, because you don't know each other yet. I can assure you that this process will help strengthen your communication and build a strong sense of respect and support. One of my favorite verses about a fight comes from Ecclesiastes 7:8-9; "Finishing is better than starting. Patience is better than pride. Don't be quick-tempered, for anger is the friend of fools."

The thing about anger is that it blinds you. It enables you to see only the negative and, often, to dwell on it ,until your eyes are bloodshot, and any rational thoughts are gone. Anger is dangerous, because it taints your view of your partner. This often happens with friends and family, too.

I had a friend who was taken back when I first introduced her to Ben. She informed me she didn't feel we were a good fit. The problem with that was when I did get in a fight with him, the memory of her words fueled my anger. I just seemed to get angrier with the situation. From my experience with fights I just want to say that, sometimes, it's impossible to completely hold your anger back, and I'm not saying to bury it. That will just lead to hurt and unresolved issues.

When you have those big fights— the moments you feel like breaking up— don't walk away. Sit down together and say nothing for a few minutes. The biggest mistakes couples make is walking away, instead of pushing through. Ben and I do not fight often, but, when we do it usually last around four hours. I'm not going to lie: there have been moments I did walk out, but all it did was leave me crying in the parking lot of his apartment complex for a few hours, cause me to lose sleep, and make it impossible to focus on anything the following day.

When women begin to spill the issue, they tend to go everywhere. We start with one thing, and, then, we bring up something from three weeks ago, or even anticipation of future problems. Don't panic. I don't know why, but, when women begin that process, they usually find the real problem. They just have to vent in order to dig it up. The best way to react to that is to wait until she is completely done and say, "Help me understand what the problem is. That was a lot for me to take in."

There are a few people who are non-confrontational and are the exception; however, this is very dangerous. People who hold it all in until it builds up often explode like a volcano when they finally blow, bringing the whole relationship down with it! If you are that person, I highly recommend you work on expressing yourself. When you're getting serious with someone and even considering marriage, you have to realize they'll be there for *everything*. Therefore…you *do not* escape them. Their annoying habits and personality quirks are permanently in your life. If something they do is hurting or eating at you…talk about it.

Most of this is common sense, but ladies often don't realize how much we overlook this step, especially in the beginning. Because of that hardwiring difference, we tend to forget that guys say a lot of things without analyzing them first. That means he will say or do something that will hurt you, and he will not notice! Girls build up the situation and get so upset over literally nothing. Don't get me wrong, ladies, I get where you're coming from as thoughts fly through your head like, "But that was disrespectful, or "He disappointed me on our anniversary," but I'll bet you he has no idea what he did to upset you.

For example, when a couple is on a budget, the couple may agree not to do anything for an anniversary. And, although it is established that you both will not do anything, *girls still expect something…* mainly a card. However, when they guy doesn't do this, you must remember the guy is not a mind reader. Be clear on what you want. I know you may think, "I want him to do it without me asking, or else it loses its meaning." Ladies, let me make this perfectly clear right now: the chick flick, Shakespeare, and romance novels are *fantasy*. No guy has ever or will ever live up to the romantic advances these amazing writers created.

Tell him what you want. I tried to wait it out once, and I lasted six weeks before I broke. Then, I erupted over everything, because I was so disappointed. It is not worth it! Just tell him.

Most important is to avoiding being an atomic bomb, which means when you are mad you become silent until you're triggered. This is the worst way to accomplish anything! Let me put it bluntly: when a soldier is in battle and he's on the field and it's quiet, there is nothing wrong. It is not until you hear gunfire, bombs, and cannons that the soldier realizes they're in the danger zone. Talk when you are angry, or when you do go off, everything will just be a mesh of emotion.

RESPECT

We all know the word respect. According to *Webster's Dictionary*, the meaning is: <u>to take notice of; to regard with special attention; to regard as worthy of special consideration; hence, to care for; to heed</u>.

That is part of it, but, in a relationship respect is more than that. 1 Thessalonians 5:11 says, "So encourage each other and build each other up, just as you are already doing." A relationship will heed balance based on respect. If there is a mutual respect, you will find the relationship is a partnership. In a partnership, both parties encourage each other and push each other. Obstacles are overcome easier, because they are conquered together. Memories are fonder because the moment is shared.

One of the best quotes to describe a relationship comes from Ecclesiastes 4:9-11; "Two people can accomplish more than twice as much as one; they get a better return for their labor. If one person falls, the other can reach out and help. But people who are alone when they fall area in real trouble. And on a cold night, two under the same blanket can gain warmth from each other. But how can one be warm alone?" (If you're single, do not be discouraged. You will find someone. Unfortunately that often only comes when you least expect it and let it go.)

To respect someone is not done by separating your roles, but it's to be a team and lift each other up. If one of you is home sick and the other works, bring home soup. If you both work, then, work as a team to make and clean dinner. Japanese philosopher Daisaku Ikeda once said, "The bottom line is that without respect, no relationship will last for very long, nor can two people bring out the best in each other."

If you have the chance read Emerson Eggerichs's Love & Respect: The Love She Most Desires; The Respect He Desperately Needs, it will open your eyes to the hardwiring differences of a men and women and how respect is given. How to show a man respect is totally different than how to show a woman respect. For both genders, receiving respect is a necessity. I highly recommend reading or watching this, especially if you are in the early stages of marriage. Eggerichs is comical, and it is super-fun to watch, as you'll poke fun at each other for these generic scenarios that are so true.

DANGER ZONE

Once insecurities are overcome, there is only one thing that will kill your relationship...comfort. This is the hardest thing to beat, because if you get married five, even ten years down the line, and you've done everything in the book, there is nothing else to do. That's fine, but realize that doesn't mean you have to stop doing stuff to show how much that person means to you.

For instance, bringing home a bouquet of flowers or making a simple dessert will never get old! Ladies, the main reason a guy cheats in a relationship is because he gets bored. Guys, the main reason women stop trying in a relationship is because she gets frustrated with the lack of effort. The hardest thing to fight is the routine a couple creates in a relationship. They hang out at the same time, eat the same dinners, watch the same movies, and pretty soon, when you meet someone fun who does something you don't do, you wonder what it would be like to be with them.

I'll let you all in on a little secret... LOVE IS HARD! It takes constant effort to maintain. If you do not choose love, you will not obtain it.

Fingerprint Series

I have a theory that has always worked for me. I look at love as a competition in which a couple is constantly competing to show each other how much the other means to them. In the competition, however, you don't keep score. If you do one something or five somethings before they get the chance to do something, that doesn't mean you love them more. If one of the two decides to stop competing, the relationship dies.

Galatians 6:9 speaks to this; "So don't get tired of doing what is good. Don't get discouraged and give up, for we will reap a harvest of blessing at the appropriate time." That verse can be applied to any situation in your life, but, when applied in a relationship, it makes perfect sense. Realistically, all couples create a routine. My husband and I always make dinner together, do dishes, and watch our favorite show. During the week, there isn't too much time, and that's understandable. To fight the routine, we go out on Friday and Saturdays. He'll plan two dates, and I'll plan two dates. Sometimes, if we don't feel like cooking, we'll drive around on the freeway, pick an off ramp, and look for a hole-in-the-wall place to eat. Is it the most exciting thing ever? No, but it takes you out of you normal, predictable routine and is just enough to add flavor.

LOVE VS. INFATUATION

The problem with today's society is our need for instant gratification. From a young age, our generation has been taught we can have anything at the click of a button: food, movies, music, games. The problem with this is that it gets applied to our desire for affection. People forget that, even though you can control every aspect of your life, you can't control someone else's life, especially their emotions.

Multiple studies in America have shown that the divorce rate is now 50 percent! People become so set on marriage and what they want to accomplish right now, they don't logically think about it. Everyone goes through an infatuation stage, which is important. That first physical attraction and curiosity is what starts a relationship.

However, people forget that everything fades away, looks go with age, and a person's personality will change your opinion as you get to know them.

Infatuation is when you see that person with perfection. Everything is funny; they can do no wrong. You are infatuated with someone if you are constantly checking Facebook, checking your phone, wanting to be with them every minute you can. Love is seeing that person for who they are and accepting them. All the quirks and all the differences.

What most people do not get is that love is a choice. You either choose to fight for your relationship, or you let it go. This goes back to the difficulty of self-discipline. Just like keeping your body fit, it requires effort and a constant steadiness to maintain. Do I feel it gets harder as it gets older? Possibly. Ben and I have been together eight years now. Many of my family members have been together over twenty-five years, and I have learned from them that communication and anticipating the other person becomes so easy because you know them. Keeping it fresh and exciting, though, is a little bit of a struggle.

FAMILY

This is the most difficult part about dating, especially if you're close with your family. Here's the thing: your family loves you and wants to protect you from anything harmful, including relationships. There is this lovely little line separating your girlfriend/boyfriend from your family. Your job is to keep it! One thing I didn't realize is that when you go home upset, when you vent to your parent, you are shaping their view of your boyfriend/girlfriend. This can be very dangerous. You need to become your own entity *before* allowing family to influence it. At the same time, though, don't ignore the wisdom your family has in buying a house, raising a child, etc.

SEX...THE DEADLY SIN

Sex is a topic that is taboo to talk about. Nowadays, it seems like every adult is determined to shove one piece of Scripture down every kids throat: that pre-marital sex is bad. The real question, though, is why? God designed sex as a gift for mankind, a sacred thing where a man and woman become one. A few aspects don't seem to get mentioned often.

First, recognize what virginity is: it is a gift God designed for a husband and wife to share a bond emotionally and physically. Virginity is also a mindset. You know how they always say ignorance is bliss... they're not kidding. Once you have sex, it is extremely difficult— practically impossible— to get away from.

The biggest thing I want to talk about is the emotional connections. Many people look poorly upon arranged marriages; however, in the Bible, when women were twelve, they were sold for goats. Surprisingly, though, the marriages usually end up lasting, because they give each other their virginity.

Giving someone that gift is also giving them an emotional attachment that is indescribable. God designed for a man and woman to share that experience, so that they become one both physically and emotionally. The emotional attachment that takes place between the couple is huge. The feelings are so strong that they carry a couple through practically any trials they encounter. Couples who save themselves usually create a uniquely unwavering dependency and respect for each other that shields them from all the what ifs.

For example, if a man marries a woman, and they give themselves to each other, chances are he's not going out wondering what he's missing out on and idolizing other women as sex toys. There is nothing sadder to me than to watch a girl give herself to a man to keep his "love"— a.k.a. attention— and all he ends up doing is abusing her from then on. I was on the cheer team, and I heard so many sad stories of girls who ran themselves all over town to try and ensure her man was happy. At the end of the day, the guy was cheating on her. I even know girls who have made that bond and stayed through cheating and STDs and abuse because she couldn't break it. High school is complicated and frustrating. It's often based on looks and how far you'll go. I know how hard it is to be shunned for being the goodie goodie, but, at the end of the day, virginity is not a disease. You gain more respect for yourself and those around you, and the person you chose to give that gift to will honor and love you for the sacrifice.

The second important thing is to know how sex is used in a relationship. Women, here is the tricky part: once you let a man have your virginity, you can't take it back. Think about the section earlier, in which we talked about how women are emotional. Well, men fulfill their emotional needs through physical contact. That's why when you hold his hand or give him a goodnight kiss, he sparks to cloud nine.

A man who hasn't been physical can enjoy the simple things, like kisses. So, when you have sex with a man, his need for sex becomes emotional security. Once that happens, if you do not continue to satisfy your man regularly, two things will occur in your relationship. First, he becomes extremely insecure. He thinks he's not good enough and becomes over-possessive or controlling, because he is looking to see if she is no longer physically attracted. Second is that because of the insecurity, he becomes uneasy in the relationship. He may even question his girl and think she is cheating. Either way you look at it, the relationship is coming to a quick end.

Women, making the decision to give your virginity to someone is huge. I don't care what anyone says: God designed you to have it, because it comes with so much more than just one action of sex.

Ladies, you are hardwired for emotion, and that can get in the way. Like I said, once a girl decides to give herself to boy, you become blinded by love, and your pain tolerance spikes to a point that is unbearable for the people who love you to watch. You think because you gave him your most sacred gift, he'll love you and treat you better. Instead, you end up dragging yourself through emotional and physiological duress for what some girls will withstand for years! I know not all relationships end up this way, but I can guarantee this: it open the doors to huge insecurities and vulnerability. It amazes me how critical a girl becomes of herself once she's had sex. She starts thinking she has to look and act a certain way, based on comments from her boyfriend. The reason sex is so warned against—besides pregnancy— is because you can become so easily influenced emotionally, and, let's face it: the average high school boy is not the best influence in any area.

Men, you're caught between a rock and a hard place. From the age of fourteen, everything in your life centers around sex. From phone apps, to television and movies, to most music lyrics, you are bombarded by sex. The hard part for you guys is that you are hardwired for sex. In biblical times, you got married at sixteen! Now, you're told wait until you get married, but when will that be?!

Just remember this: ignorance is bliss. Once you open Pandora's Box, there is no going back. The devil is sly, and he knows the raging hormones you get! Nowadays, it has become so much easier for the devil to attck you. You may think, "I'll just look at porn. No one's looking," or, "Just buy a Playboy magazine. No one will know." Slowly, it becomes a daily battle.

If a man is not mature enough to handle the commitment of sex, two major things happen. First, your girlfriend becomes a play toy. You completely lose sight of her as a person, and, now, it's suddenly about what you can get from her. Second, girls become a game. You're constantly looking for the scoreboard and rating every girl. Friends become competition, and you find yourself going so far as to make up lies about your sexual escapades, trying to outdo each other. Your view of the world is tainted by everything physical, and you lose sight of what a relationship in God is. Be careful of how quick you want to lose your V-card. In the end, a woman likes a man who knows what he wants and has the ability to control himself.

For those who have already had sex. Are you condemned to hell? Not if you have repented. I'm not a fire-and-brimstone type of girl, so this is all I really want to say: sex is designed for a reason, and it is even called "making love" for a reason. Once a couple has created a strong emotional foundation in God and shares that bond, sex is designed to change your mindset and heart to care, love, and protect that person through everything. Those people who go around attempting to find love and fulfillment through sex will always end up lonely at the end of the day. Value your body and heart, and save it for someone you really love and will love you back…forever.

God has an amazing plan for your life. He has called you to be different, loved, and joyful. Life is complicated and hard prise. What is amazing is how when you embrace God in your life, seek Him, give the Holy Spirit control, and lean on Him in your trials, it becomes so much easier. You can spend your whole life looking for fulfillment and never find it. God makes it so simple, yet we complicate it with our expectations and formulas. Don't become a victim of culture or religion. Fight to know God, and everything else will fall into place. God is incredible, indescribable, and all-powerful. He is ALWAYS in control, and He has a particular design just for you!

DAILY INSPIRATIONS

- *To be comfortable with someone you must first be comfortable with you*
- *Don't be a victim of identity theft*
- *Comfort is nice, but paralyzing*
- *Anger only lets you see the negative*
- *Constantly show your spouse you love them*

REFLECTIONS

What activities do you do to keep your foundation strong?

Do you both communicate well in a fight?

What have you done to show your love to your spouse?

CPSIA information can be obtained
at www.ICGtesting.com
Printed in the USA
FSHW04n1610280318
46015FS